AUTOGRAPHS FOR FREEDOM
(VOLUME I)

LECTOR HOUSE PUBLIC DOMAIN WORKS

This book is a result of an effort made by Lector House towards making a contribution to the preservation and repair of original classic literature. The original text is in the public domain in the United States of America, and possibly other countries depending upon their specific copyright laws.

In an attempt to preserve, improve and recreate the original content, certain conventional norms with regard to typographical mistakes, hyphenations, punctuations and/or other related subject matters, have been corrected upon our consideration. However, few such imperfections might not have been rectified as they were inherited and preserved from the original content to maintain the authenticity and construct, relevant to the work. The work might contain a few prior copyright references as well as page references which have been retained, wherever considered relevant to the part of the construct. We believe that this work holds historical, cultural and/or intellectual importance in the literary works community, therefore despite the oddities, we accounted the work for print as a part of our continuing effort towards preservation of literary work and our contribution towards the development of the society as a whole, driven by our beliefs.

We are grateful to our readers for putting their faith in us and accepting our imperfections with regard to preservation of the historical content. We shall strive hard to meet up to the expectations to improve further to provide an enriching reading experience.

Though, we conduct extensive research in ascertaining the status of copyright before redeveloping a version of the content, in rare cases, a classic work might be incorrectly marked as not-in-copyright. In such cases, if you are the copyright holder, then kindly contact us or write to us, and we shall get back to you with an immediate course of action.

HAPPY READING!

AUTOGRAPHS FOR FREEDOM
(VOLUME I)

VARIOUS, JULIA GRIFFITHS

ISBN: 978-93-90294-24-4

Published: 1853

© 2020
LECTOR HOUSE LLP

LECTOR HOUSE LLP
E-MAIL: lectorpublishing@gmail.com

'HE IS NOT ASHAMED TO CALL THEM BRETHREN.'

AUTOGRAPHS FOR FREEDOM (VOLUME I)

BY

VARIOUS

EDITED BY
JULIA GRIFFITHS.

IN TWO VOLUMES,
VOL. I.

1853.

PREFACE.

THERE is, perhaps, little need of detaining the kind reader, even for one moment, in this the vestibule of our Temple of Liberty, to state the motives and reasons for the publication of this collection of Anti-slavery testimonies.

The good cause to which the volume is devoted;—the influence which must ever be exerted by persons of exalted character, and high mental endowments;—the fact that society is slow to accept any cause that has not the baptism of the acknowledged noble and good;—the happiness arising from making any exertion to ameliorate the condition of the injured race amongst us, will, at once, suggest reasons and motives for sending forth this offering, which, while it shall prove acceptable as a GIFT BOOK, may help to swell the tide of that sentiment that, by the Divine blessing, will sweep away from this otherwise happy land, the great sin of SLAVERY.

Should this publication be instrumental in casting *one* ray of hope on the heart of one poor slave, or should it draw the attention of one person, hitherto uninterested, to the deep wrongs of the bondman, or cause one sincere and earnest effort to promote emancipation, we believe that the kind contributors, who have generously responded to our call, not less than the members of our Society, will feel themselves gratified and compensated.

The proceeds of the sale of the "AUTOGRAPHS FOR FREEDOM," will be devoted to the dissemination of light and truth on the subject of slavery throughout the country.

On behalf of *"The Rochester Ladies' Anti-Slavery Society,"*

JULIA GRIFFITHS, *Secretary.*

ROCHESTER, 1852.

CONTENTS

Page

- PREFACE. vi
- BE UP AND DOING.. 1
  Hon. William H. Seward.
- CASTE AND CHRIST. 3
  Mrs. H. E. B. Stowe.
- LETTER FROM THE EARL OF CARLISLE TO THE SECRETARY OF THE SOCIETY. 5
  Carlisle
- MOMMA CHARLOTTE. 8
  Mrs. C. M. Kirkland
- A NAME, ... 11
  Hon. Horace Mann.
- TO THE SECRETARY OF THE SOCIETY.. 12
  Joseph Sturge
- SLAVERY AND POLYGAMY: DOCTORS OF DIVINITY IN A DILEMMA. 13
  R. Hildreth
- THE WAY.. 15
  John G. Whittier
- THE SLAVE AND SLAVE-OWNER. 16
  Miss C M Sedgwick

- LETTER FROM THE BISHOP OF OXFORD TO THE SECRETARY OF THE SOCIETY. 18
  Samuel Wilberforce

- "HIDE THE OUTCASTS."..................19
  Rev. Wm Goodell

- CAN SLAVES RIGHTFULLY RESIST AND FIGHT?..............21
  Rev. Geo. W. Perkins

- DEATH IN LIFE..................25
  Ebenezer Button..

- TRUE REFORM..................26
  Mrs Caroline W. Healey Dall.

- HOW LONG?..................28
  J. M. Whitfield.

- LETTER FROM WILSON ARMISTEAD TO THE SECRETARY OF THE SOCIETY..................34
  Wilson Armistead

- IMPROMPTU STANZAS,..................36
  J. M. Eells.

- JOHN MURRAY (OF GLASGOW)...................38
  James M'Cune Smith

- POWER OF AMERICAN EXAMPLE..................41
  Lewis Tappan.

- "THE GOSPEL AS A REMEDY FOR SLAVERY."..................43
  Lewis Tappan

- LETTER TO THE PRESIDENT OF THE SOCIETY...................45
  C. G. Finney

- THE SLAVE'S PRAYER..................46
  Miss Catharine E. Beecher.

CONTENTS

- THE STRUGGLE.. 47
    Hon. Charles Sumner

- WORK AND WAIT. 48
    Horace Greeley

- THE GREAT EMANCIPATION. 50
    Gerrit Smith

- ODE 51
    Rev. John Pierpont

- PASSAGES IN THE LIFE OF A SLAVE WOMAN. 54
    Annie Parker.

- STORY TELLING. 59
    Annie Parker.

- THE MAN-OWNER.. 61
    Rev. E. Buckingham

- DAMASCUS IN 1851. 64
    Rev. F W Holland

- RELIGIOUS, MORAL, AND POLITICAL DUTIES. 68
    Lindley Murray Moore.

- WHY SLAVERY IS IN THE CONSTITUTION. 69
    James G. Birney.

- THE TWO ALTARS; 74
    Mrs. H. B. Stowe.

- OUTLINE OF A MAN.. 84
    Rev. Robt. R. Raymond

- THE HEROIC SLAVE-WOMAN.. 91
    Rev. Samuel J. May

- KOSSUTH. 93
    John Thomas

- THE HEROIC SLAVE. 97
  Frederick Douglass.

- A PLEA FOR FREE SPEECH. 126
  Prof. J. H. Raymond

- PLACIDO. 133
  Prof. William G. Allen

BE UP AND DOING.

Can nothing be done for Freedom? Yes, much can be done. Everything can be done. Slavery can be confined within its present bounds. It can be meliorated. It can be, and it must be abolished. The task is as simple as its performance would be beneficent and as its rewards would be glorious. It requires only that we follow this plain rule of conduct and course of activity, namely, to do, everywhere, and on every occasion what we can, and not to neglect nor refuse to do what we can at any time, because at that precise time and on that particular occasion we cannot do more. Circumstances define possibilities. When we have done our best to shape them and to make them propitious, we may rest satisfied that superior wisdom has, nevertheless, controlled them and us, and that it will be satisfied with us if we do all the good that shall then be found possible.

But we can, and we must begin deeper and lower than the composition and combination of factions. Wherein do the security and strength of slavery consist? You answer, in the constitution of the United States, and in the constitutions and laws of the slave-holding States. Not at all. It is in the erroneous sentiments of the American people. Constitutions and laws can no more rise above the virtue of the people than the limpid stream can climb above its native spring. Inculcate the love of freedom and the sacredness of the rights of man under the paternal roof. See to it, that they are taught in the schools and in the churches. Reform your own codes and expurgate the vestiges of slavery. Reform your own manners and customs and rise above the prejudices of caste. Receive the fugitive who lays his weary limbs at your door, and defend him as you would your household gods, for he, not they, has power to bring down blessings on your hearth. Correct your error that slavery has any constitutional guarantee that may not be released, and that ought not to be relinquished. Say to slavery, when it shows its bond and demands its pound of flesh, that if it draws one drop of blood its life shall pay the forfeit. Inculcate that the free States can exercise the rights of hospitality and humanity, that Congress knows no finality and can debate, that Congress can at least mediate with the slave-holding States, that at least future generations may be bought and given up to freedom. Do all this, and inculcate all this, in the spirit of moderation and benevolence, and not of retaliation and fanaticism, and you will ultimately bring the parties of this country into a common condemnation and even the slave-holding States themselves into a renunciation of slavery, which is not less necessary for them than for the common security and welfare. Whenever the public mind shall be prepared, and the public conscience shall demand the abolition of slavery the way to do it will open before us, and then mankind will be surprised at the ease with which the greatest of social and political evils can be removed.

Hon. William H. Seward.

CASTE AND CHRIST.

He is not ashamed to call them brethren.

Ho! thou dark and weary stranger
From the tropic's palmy strand,
Bowed with toil, with mind benighted,
What wouldst thou upon our land?

Am I not, O man, thy brother?
Spake the stranger patiently,
All that makes thee, man, immortal,
Tell me, dwells it not in me?

I, like thee, have joy, have sorrow,
I, like thee, have love and fear,
I, like thee, have hopes and longings
Far beyond this earthly sphere.

Thou art happy,—I am sorrowing,
Thou art rich, and I am poor;
In the name of our *one* Father
Do not spurn me from your door.

Thus the dark one spake, imploring,
To each stranger passing nigh,
But each child and man and woman,
Priest and Levite passed him by.

Spurned of men,—despised, rejected,
Spurned from school and church and hall,
Spurned from business and from pleasure,
Sad he stood, apart from all.

Then I saw a form all glorious,
Spotless as the dazzling light,
As He passed, men veiled their faces,
And the earth, as heaven, grew bright.

Spake he to the dusky stranger,
Awe-struck there on bended knee,
Rise! for *I* have called thee *brother*,
I am not ashamed of thee.

When I wedded mortal nature

To my Godhead and my throne,
Then I made all mankind sacred,
Sealed all human for mine own.

By Myself, the Lord of ages,
I have sworn to right the wrong,
I have pledged my word, unbroken,
For the weak against the strong.

And upon my gospel banner
I have blazed in light the sign,
He who scorns his lowliest brother,
Never shall have hand of mine.

Hear the word!—who fight for freedom!
Shout it in the battle's van!
Hope! for bleeding human nature!
Christ the *God*, is Christ the *man*!

Mrs. H. E. B. Stowe.

ANDOVER, JULY 22, 1852.

LETTER FROM THE EARL OF CARLISLE TO THE SECRETARY OF THE SOCIETY.

London, July 8, 1852.

Madam:—

I should be very sorry indeed to refuse any request addressed to me from "the Rochester Ladies' Anti-Slavery Association."

At the same time I really should feel at a loss what to send, but as I am on the point of sending off a letter to the authoress of Uncle Tom's Cabin, I venture to submit a copy of it to those who I feel sure must be fond of such a countrywoman.

Your very faithful Servant,

Carlisle

London, July 8, 1852.

Madam:—

I have allowed some time to elapse before I thanked you for the great honor and kindness you did me in sending to me, from yourself, a copy of Uncle Tom's Cabin. I thought it due to the subject of which I perceived that it treated, not to send a mere acknowledgment, as I confess from a motive of policy I am apt to do, upon the first arrival of the book. I therefore determined to read, before I wrote.

Having thus read, it is not in the stiff and conventional form of compliment, still less in the technical language of criticism, that I am about to speak of your work. I return my deep and solemn thanks to Almighty God, who has led and enabled you to write such a book.

I do feel, indeed, the most thorough assurance that in His good providence such a book cannot have been written in vain. I have long felt that slavery is by far the *topping* question of the world and age we live in, involving all that is most thrilling in heroism, and most touching in distress,—in short, the real epic of the universe. The self-interest of the parties most nearly concerned on the one hand, the apathy and ignorance of unconcerned observers on the other, have left these august pretensions to drop very much out of sight, and hence my rejoicing that a writer has appeared who will be read, and must be felt, and that happen what may to the transactions of slavery, they will no longer be suppressed, "carent quia vate sacrâ."

I trust that what I have just said was not required to show the entire sympathy I entertain with respect to the main truth and leading scope of your high argument, but we live in a world only too apt to regard the accessories and accidents of a subject above its real and vital essence; no one can know so well as you how much the external appearance of the negro detracts from the romance and sentimentality which undoubtedly might attach to his position and his wrongs, and on this account it does seem to me proportionately important that you should have brought to your portraiture great grace of style, great power of language, a play of humor which relieves and brightens even the dark depth of the background which you were called upon to reveal, a force of pathos which, to give it the highest praise, does not lay behind even all the dread reality, and, above all, a variety, a discrimination, and a truth in the delineation of character, which even to my own scanty and limited experience of the society you describe accredits itself instantaneously and irresistibly. Seldom, indeed, could I more forcibly apply the line of a very favorite poet,—

"And truths divine came mended from that tongue."

I have been told that in an English periodical, the quality of genius has been denied to your book. The motives which must have guided its composition will probably have made you supremely indifferent to mere criticism, especially to any which argues so much obfuscation both of head and heart. Your work has genius of the highest order, and it is the lowest of its merits.

There is one point which, in face of all that your book has aimed at and achieved, I think of extremely slight importance, but which I will nevertheless just mention, if only to show that I have not been bribed into this fervor of admiration. I think, then, that whenever you speak of England and her institutions, it is in a tone which fails to do them fair justice. I do not know what distinct charges you think could be established against our aristocracy and capitalists, but you generally convey the impression that the same oppressions in degree, though not in kind, might be brought home to them which are now laid to the charge of Southern slave-holders. Exposed to the same ordeal, they might very probably not stand the test better. All I contend for is, that the circumstances in which they are placed, and the institutions by which they are surrounded, make the parallel wholly inapplicable. I cannot but suspect that your view has been in many respects derived from composers of fiction and others among ourselves who, writing with distinguished ability, have been more successful in delineating and dissecting the morbid features of our modern society, than in detecting the principle which is at fault, or suggesting the appropriate remedy. My own belief is, liable, if you please, to national bias, that our capitalists are very much the same sort of persons as your own in the Northern States, with the same mixtures and inequalities of motive and action. With respect to our aristocracy, I should really be tempted to say that, tried by their conduct on the question of Free Trade, they do not sustain an unfavorable comparison with your uppermost classes. Allow me to add, that when in one place you refer to those who have already emancipated their slaves, I think a case more directly in point than the proceedings of the Hungarian nobles might have been selected: such, at least, I feel sure would have been the case, if the passages in question had been written by one who certainly was keenly alive to the faults of England, but who did justice to her good qualities and deeds with a heartiness exceeding that of most of her own sons,—your great and good Dr. Channing.

I need not repeat how irrelevant, after all, I feel what I have said upon this head to be to the main issues involved in your work; there is little doubt, too, that as a nation we have our special failings, and one of them probably is that we care too little about what other nations think of them.

Nor can I wish my countrymen ever to forget that their own past history should prevent them from being forward in casting accusations on their transatlantic brethren on the subject of slavery. With great ignorance of its actual miseries and horrors, there is also among us great ignorance of the fearful perplexities and difficulties with which its solution could not fail to be attended. I feel, however, that there is a considerable difference between reluctant acquiescence in what you inherit from the past, and voluntary fresh enlargements and reinforcements of the system. For instance, I should not say that the mode in which such an enactment as the Fugitive Slave Law has been considered in this country has at all erred upon the side of overmuch indignation.

I need not detain you longer: I began my letter with returning thanks to Almighty God for the appearance of your work, and I offer my humble and ardent prayer to the same Supreme Source that it may have a marked agency in hastening the great consummation, which I should feel it a practical atheism not to believe must be among the unfulfilled purposes of the Divine power and love.

I have the honor to be, Madam,
Your sincere admirer and well-wisher,
CARLISLE.

Mrs. Beecher Stowe.

MOMMA CHARLOTTE.

"Slavery is merely an idea!" said Mr. S— —; "the slaves are, in reality, better off than we are, if they had sense enough to know it. They are taken care of—(they must be, you know, because it is the master's interest to keep them in good condition, and a man will always do what is for his interest). They get rid of all responsibility,—which is what we are groaning under; and if they were only let alone, they would be happy enough,—happier than their masters, I dare say."

"You think it, then, anything but kindness to urge their emancipation?"

"To be sure I do! and I would have every one that teaches them to be discontented hung up without judge or jury."

"You seem particularly interested for the slave,—"

"Interested! I would have every one of them sent beyond the Rocky Mountains, if I could,—or into 'kingdom come,' for that matter. They are the curse of the country; but as long as they are *property*, I would shoot any man that put bad ideas in their heads or that interfered with my management of them, as I would shoot a dog that killed my sheep."

"But do they never get what you call 'bad ideas' from any but white people?"

"O, there is no knowing where they get them,—but they are full of 'em. No matter how kind you are to them, they are never satisfied!"

"I can tell you where they get some of their ideas of slavery, if you will allow me."

"Certainly,—I am always glad of information."

"Well,—I will take up your time with nothing but actual facts, for the truth of which I will be answerable. In a Western tour, not many years since, I saw one day a young lady, fair as a lily, and with a sweet expression of countenance, walking in the street with a little black girl whom she held by the hand. The little girl was about six years old, neatly dressed and very clean; and on her neck she had a little gauze shawl that somebody had given her, the border of which was composed of the figure of the American Eagle many times repeated, each impression accompanied by the word 'Liberty,' woven into the fabric.

"This curious decoration, together with the wistful look of the child's face, and the benevolent air of the young lady, with whom I was slightly acquainted, led me to ask some questions, which were answered with an air in which modesty and sensibility were blended. I learned that the young lady had undertaken the trying task of accompanying the little girl through the place—which was a considerable village—for the purpose of collecting the sum of fifty dollars, with which to purchase the freedom of the child.

"'And how,' said I, 'did you become interested in the poor little thing?'

"'She belongs to a member of my family,' said Miss C— —, with a blush; 'to my aunt, Mrs. Jones.'

"'And how did she find her way to the north?'

"'Her mother, who is the servant of my aunt, got leave to bring Violet along with her, when her mistress came here for the summer.'

"'But both mother and child are free by the mere circumstance of being brought here,—'

"'O, but Momma Charlotte promised her mistress that she would not leave her, nor let Violet do so, if she might bring the child with her, and beg money to buy her. She says she does not care for freedom for herself.'

"I could not do less than go with the good girl for awhile, to assist a little in her labor of love, which in the end, and with a good deal of difficulty, was finally accomplished. It was not until after this that I became acquainted with Momma Charlotte, the mother of Violet, and learned a few of the particulars of a story which had made her 'not care for freedom.'

"Momma Charlotte was the mother of ten children,—six daughters and four sons. Her husband had been a free black,—a carpenter, able to keep a comfortable home for his family, hiring his wife of her master. At the time of the Southampton insurrection, this man was among the suspected, and, on suspicion, not proof, he was taken up,—tried, after the fashion of that time, and hung, with several others,—all between sunset and sunrise of a single day.

"'He was innocent,—he had had no hand in the matter, as God is my judge!' said poor Momma Charlotte.

"This was but the beginning of troubles. A sense of insecurity made the sale of slaves more vigorous than ever. Charlotte's children were sold, one by one—no two together—the boys for the sugar country,—the girls for—'the New Orleans market,' whence they were dispersed, she never knew where.

"'All gone!' she said; 'where I could never see 'em nor hear from 'em. I don't even know where one of 'em is!'

"'And Violet?'

"'O yes,—I mean all but Violet. She's all I've got in the world, and I want to keep her. I begged Missus to let me keep jist one! and she said if I could get any body to buy her for me, I might have her,—for you know I couldn't own her myself, 'cause I'm a slave.'

"'But you are no longer a slave, Momma Charlotte; your mistress by bringing you here voluntarily has freed you,—'

"'Yes,—I know,—but I promised, you see! And I don't care to be free. I'm old, and my children's gone, and my heart's broke. I ha'n't no more courage. If I can keep Violet, it's all I expect. My mistress is good enough to me,—I live pretty easy.'

"Such was Momma Charlotte's philosophy, but her face told through what sufferings such philosophy had been acquired. A fixed grief sat on her brow; since the judicial murder of her husband she had never been known to laugh,—hardly to smile. Her eyes were habitually cast on the ground, and her voice seemed always on the brink of tears. She was what you call '*dissatisfied*,' I think, Mr. S——."

"O, you have selected an extreme case! those things very seldom happen." (Seldom!) "After all, you see the poor old thing knew what was right; she showed the right spirit,—"

"Yes,—she,—but her *owners*?"

Here Mr. S—— was sure he saw a friend at a distance to whom it was necessary he should speak immediately; so he darted off, and I lost the benefit of his defence of the peculiarities of the peculiar institution.

Mrs C. M. Kirkland

Mrs. C. M. Kirkland

A NAME,

ON BEING ASKED FOR HIS AUTOGRAPH.

Why ask a Name? Small is the good it brings;
Names are but breath; *deeds*, DEEDS alone are Things.

Horace Mann,

Hon. Horace Mann.

WEST NEWTON, OCT. 23, 1852.

TO THE SECRETARY OF THE SOCIETY.

IN compliance with the request that I would send a few lines for insertion in "The Anti-Slavery Autograph," I may say that I cannot express too strongly my conviction that, if there be truth in Revelation, it is the duty of every Christian to promote, by all legitimate means, not only the universal and total, but the *immediate* abolition of any system under which man can hold property in his fellow man. Perhaps few of those who take this view of the subject are sufficiently careful to avoid, as far as possible, any participation in, or encouragment of slavery, by refusing to use the produce of the unrequited toil of the slave. Yet until we do this, I think we have little right to expect the Divine blessing upon our efforts to promote the abolition of slavery and of the slave trade.

Joseph Sturge

SLAVERY AND POLYGAMY: DOCTORS OF DIVINITY IN A DILEMMA.

An argument is derived from the Jewish Scriptures in favor of slave-holding, very plausible and weighty with that large class of persons so poorly gifted with hearts as to find it difficult to discriminate between the letter that killeth and the spirit that maketh alive. The Old Testament shows clearly enough, that slave-holding was tolerated among the Jews; and it being assumed that the system of Jewish society, or, at all events, that the Mosaic code was framed after a Divine model, it is alleged to be at least supererogatory, if not actually impious, to denounce as inconsistent with Christianity that which God permitted to his chosen and selected people. Are *we* to pretend to be better and wiser than Abraham and Moses, David and Solomon?

A recent application of this same argument can hardly fail to operate with many, as what the mathematicians call a *reductio ad absurdum*; a proof, that is, of the falsity of a proposition assumed, by exhibiting its operation in other cases.

The famous Mormon doctrine of the plurality of wives, now at length openly avowed by the heads and apostles of that new sect, is upheld and justified by this very same argument. It plainly appears from the Old Testament, that polygamy equally with slavery, was one of the social institutions of the Jews, recognized and sanctioned by their laws. And borrowing the tone, and indeed the very words of our pro-slavery theologians,—"Do you pretend," asks Orson Hyde, one of the Mormon apostles, addressing himself to those who question this new privilege of the saints—"Do you pretend to set yourselves above the teaching of God, and the example of his chosen people?"

Nor does the analogy between the two cases stop here. According to the pro-slavery biblical argument, slave-holding is only to be justified in Christian slave-holders, who, in holding slaves, have in view not only selfish benefit or advantage, but the good of the slaves, (who are not able to take care of themselves,) and the glory of God. According to the Mormon biblical argument, polygamy is to be allowed only to the saints; and that, not for any sensual gratification, but only for the benefit of the women, (who, according to the Mormon doctrine, cannot get to heaven without some holy husband to introduce them,) and for the raising up of a righteous seed to God's glory.

Their favorite biblical argument, urged with such a tone of triumph and self-satisfaction in all the southern presbyteries and consociations, and in some northern ones, being thus newly applied by the Mormons, our pro-slavery friends are placed in a somewhat delicate dilemma. For they must either abandon as invalid their dogma of slave-holding derived from Jewish practices, or, if they still hold on to the argument, and maintain its force, they must prepare to extend the right hand of fellowship to Brigham Young and his five and forty wives. It is, indeed, very natural, in fact inevitable, that slavery and polygamy, avowed or disavowed, should go together; nor does any good reason appear why those who find justification for the one in the Jewish Scriptures should hesitate about accepting the other.

R. Hildreth

THE WAY.

Believe me still, as I have ever been,
The steadfast lover of my fellow men;
My weakness,—love of holy Liberty!
My crime,—the wish that all mankind were free!
Free, not by blood; redeemed, but not by crime;
Each fetter broken, but in God's good time!

John G. Whittier

Amesbury, 10th MO. 16, 1852.

THE SLAVE AND SLAVE-OWNER.

"I WOULD rather be anything than a slave,—except a slave-owner!" said a wise and good man. The slave-owner inflicts wrongs,—the slave but suffers it. He has friends and champions by thousands. Some men live only to defend and save him. Many are willing to fight for him. Some even to die for him.

The most effective romance of our times has been written for slaves. The genius of more than one of our best poets has been consecrated to them. They divide the hearts and councils of our great nation. They are daily remembered in the prayers of the faithful. They are the most earnest topic of the christian world.

But the slave-owner! who weeps, who prays, who lives, who dies for him! True, he is of the boasted Saxon race, or descended from the brilliant Gaul, or gifted Celt. He is enriched by the transmitted civilization of all ages. He has been nurtured by christian institutions. To him have been opened the fountains of Divine truth. But from this elevation he is to be dragged down by the mill-stone of slavery.

If he be a rural landlord, he looks around upon his ancestral possessions, and sees the curse of slave-ownership upon them,—he knows the time must come when "the field shall yield no meat, the flock shall be cut off from the fold, and there shall be no herd in the stall." To him the onward tendencies of the age are reversed. His movement is steadily backward.

To the slave are held out the rewards of fortitude, of long suffering, of meekness, of patience in tribulation. What and where are the promises to the slave-owner?

Thousands among them are in a false position. They are the involuntary maintainers of wrong, and transmitters of evil. Hundreds among them have scrupulous consciences and tender feelings. They use power gently. They feed their servants bountifully. They nurse the sick kindly,—and devote weary days to their instruction. But alas! they live under the laws of slave-owners. They are forbidden to teach the slave to read, write, or cipher, to give them the means of independent progress and increasing light. Their teaching is as bootless as the labor of Sysyphus! most wearisome and disheartening.

The great eras of domestic life, bright to the thoughtless slave, are dark with forecasting shadows to the slave-owner. The mother cannot forget her sorrows, because a man-child is born. If she dare contemplate his future, she sees that the activities of his nature must be repressed, his faculties but half developed, his passions stimulated by irresponsible power, inflamed by temptation, and solicited by convenient opportunity. She knows that his path in life must be more and more entangled as he goes onward,—darker and darker with the ever-deepening misery of this cruel institution.

Is it a "*merry* marriage-bell" that rings in the ear of a slave-owning mother for the bridal of her daughter? Does not her soul recoil from the possible (probable?) evils before her child; to be placed, perchance, on an isolated plantation, environed by natural enemies; to see, it may be, the brothers and sisters of her own children follow their slave-mother to the field, or severed from her to be sold at the slave-market?

Compared with these miseries of the slave-owner, what are the toils and stripes of the slave? what his labor without stimulus or requital? what his degradation to a chattel? what the deprivation of security to the ties of kindred, and the annulling of that relation which is their source and chiefest blessing?

The slave looks forward with ever-growing hope to the struggle that must come. He joyfully "smells the battle afar off." The slave-owner folds his arms, and shuts his eyes in paralyzing despair. He hears the fearful threatenings of the gathering storm. He knows it must come,—to him fatally. It is only a question of time!

Who would not "rather be a slave than a slave-owner?"

Miss C M Sedgwick

LETTER FROM THE BISHOP OF OXFORD[1] TO THE SECRETARY OF THE SOCIETY.

CUDDELDON PALACE, JULY 7, 1852.

MADAM:—

I readily comply with your desire. England taught her descendants in America to injure their African brethren. Every Englishman should aid the American to get rid of this cleaving wrong and deep injury to his race and nation.

I am ever yours,

[signature]

Samuel Wilberforce

---

[1] A son of that distinguished friend of humanity WILLIAM WILBERFORCE.

"HIDE THE OUTCASTS."

Hide the outcasts, and bewray not
Him that wand'reth to be free;
Haste!—deliver and delay not;—
Let my outcasts dwell with thee.[2]

Shelter thou shalt not refuse him,
Lest, with him, his Lord ye slight;[3]
When, at noon, the foe pursues him,
Make thy shadow dark as night.

With thee shall he dwell, protected,
Near thee, cherished by thy side;
Though degraded, scorned, neglected,—
Thrust him not away, in pride.[4]

As, in truth, ye would that others
Unto you should succor lend,
So, to them, as equal brothers,
Equal love and help extend.[5]

Thou shalt not the slave deliver
To his master, when he flees:—
Heritage, from God, the Giver,
Yield them freely, where they please.[6]

As thyself,[7]—thy babes,—their mother,—

---

[2] "Take counsel, execute judgment; make thy shadow as the night in the midst of the noonday; hide the outcasts; bewray not him that wandereth. Let my outcasts dwell with thee, Moab; be thou a covert to them, from the face of the spoiler." Isaiah 16: 3, 4.

[3] "Inasmuch as ye did it not to one of the least of these, ye did it not to me."—*Jesus Christ*. Matt. 25: 45.

[4] "Is it not that thou deal thy bread to the hungry, and that thou bring the poor that are cast out to thy house? when thou seest the naked that thou cover him? and that thou hide not thyself from thine own flesh?" "If thou take away from the midst of thee the yoke, the putting forth of the finger, and speaking of vanity," etc. Isa. 58: 6-9.

[5] "Therefore, all things whatsoever ye would that men should do to you, do ye even so to them; for this is the law and the prophets."—*Jesus Christ*. Matt. 7: 12.

[6] "Thou shalt not deliver unto his master, the servant which is escaped from his master unto thee. He shall dwell with thee; even among you in that place which he shall choose, in one of thy gates, where it liketh him best; thou shalt not oppress him." Deut. 23: 15, 16.

[7] "Thou shalt love thy neighbor as thyself." Lev. 19: 18. Matt. 19: 19.

Thou wouldst shield from murd'rous arm,
So the slave, thy equal brother,
And his household, shield from harm.

Hearken, ye that know and fear me,[8]
Ye who in my law delight;
Ye that seek me, and revere me,
Hate the wrong, and love the right.[9]

Fear ye not, when men upbraid you,
Worms shall all their strength devour;
My salvation still shall aid you,
Coming ages learn my power.

Why forget the Lord thy Maker?
Why th' oppressor's fury dread?
Zion's King shall ne'er forsake her;—
Where's th' oppressor's fury fled?[10]

Scorn the mandates of transgressors;[11]
Fear thy God, and fear none other;
'Gainst *thyself* conspire oppressors,
When they bid thee bind thy *brother*.

Lo! the captive exile hasteth
To be loosed from thrall, forever;[12]
Lo! the power of tyrants wasteth,
Perished soon,—recovered, never!

Rev. Wm Goodell

---

[8] "Hearken unto me, ye that know righteousness; the people in whose heart is my law: fear ye not the reproach of men, neither be ye afraid of their revilings. For the moth shall eat them up like a garment, and the worm shall eat them like wool; but my righteousness shall be forever, and my salvation from generation to generation." Isaiah 51: 7, 8.

[9] "Ye that love the Lord, hate evil." Ps. 97: 10. "The fear of the Lord is to hate evil." Prov. 8: 13.

[10] "Who art thou, that thou shouldst be afraid of a man? * * * And forgettest the Lord thy Maker, * * * and hast feared continually every day, because of the fury of the oppressor, as if he were ready to destroy? And where is the fury of the oppressor?" Isaiah 51: 12, 13, 14.

[11] "We ought to obey God rather than men." Acts 5: 29.

[12] "The captive exile hasteth that he may be loosed," etc. Isaiah 51: 15.

CAN SLAVES RIGHTFULLY RESIST AND FIGHT?

I do not answer this question. But the following facts are submitted as containing the materials for an answer.

About seventy years ago, three millions of people in America thought themselves wronged by the powers ordained of God. They resolved not to endure the wrong. They published to the world a statement of grievances which justified resistance to the powers ordained of God, and deliberately revolted against the king, though explicitly commanded by God to "honor the king." In the process of revolt, about one hundred thousand men, Europeans and Americans,—were slaughtered in battle, or slowly butchered by the sickness, imprisonments, and hardships incident to a state of war.

It was distinctly maintained in 1776, that men may rightfully fight for liberty, and resist the powers ordained of God, if those powers destroyed liberty. Christian men, ministers in their pulpits strenuously argued that it was men's *duty* to fight for liberty, and to kill those who opposed them. Prayer was offered to God for success in this process of resistance and blood; and good men implored and obtained help from other nations, to complete the work of resistance to oppression, and death to the oppressors.

I do not say that these positions were right, or that the men of 1776 acted right. But I do say, that *if* they were right, we are necessarily led to some startling conclusions. For there are now three millions of people of America grievously wronged by the government they live under. *If* it was right in 1776 to resist, fight, and kill, to secure liberty,—it is right to do the same in 1852. *If* three millions of whites might rightfully resist the powers ordained of God, then three millions of blacks may rightfully do the same. *If* France was justified in aiding our band of revolutionists to fight for liberty, then a foreign nation may lawfully aid men now to vindicate their rights. *If*, as the men of 1776 declared, "when a long train of abuses evinces a design to reduce them *under absolute despotism*, it is their right, it is their *duty*, to throw off such government,"—then it is the duty of three millions of men in 1852, to throw off the government which reduces them to the frightful and absolute despotism of chattel slavery.

But what were the oppressions, which, in 1776, justified revolt, battle, and one hundred thousand deaths? They are stated in the "Declaration of Independence," are familiar to all, and will therefore only be abridged here. The powers ordained of God over the men of 1776,—"restrained their trade,"—"refused assent to laws enacted by the local legislature," — "kept soldiers to overawe them," — "did not punish soldiers for killing a few colonists," — "imposed taxes without their consent," — "in some cases, did not allow them trial by jury," — "abolished good laws," — "made war on them, in case of disobedience."

These were the wrongs they complained of. But nearly all their rights were untouched. They had schools and colleges, and could educate their children; they could become intelligent and learned themselves; they could acquire property, and large numbers of them had become rich; they could emigrate without hindrance to any other country, when weary of the oppressions of their own; they could elect their own town and state officers; they could keep swords, muskets, powder and ball in their own houses; they could not be lashed and sold like brutes; they were never compelled to work without wages; they could appeal to courts of justice for protection.

Let us now hear a statement of the wrongs inflicted on three millions of Americans in 1852.

We have no rights left to us.

Laws forbid us to be taught even to read, and severe penalties are inflicted on those who teach us.

The natural right of the parent over the child is wholly taken away; our children are systematically kept in profound ignorance, and are worked or sold like brutes, at the will of slave-holders.

We can acquire no property, and are kept in utter and perpetual pauperism, dependent on the mere caprice or selfishness of other men for subsistence.

If we attempt peaceably to emigrate from this land of oppression, we are hunted by bull-dogs, or shot down like beasts,—dragged back to perpetual slavery without trial by jury.

We are exposed to the most degrading and revolting punishments, without judge or trial, at the passion, caprice, or cruelty of the basest overseers.

When our wives and daughters are seduced or ravished, we are forbidden to appeal to the courts of justice.

Whatever outrage may be perpetrated on ourselves or our families, we have no redress.

We are compelled to work without wages; the fruits of our labor are systematically extorted from us.

Many thousands of our people are annually collected by slave-traders, and sold to distant States; by which means families are broken up, and the most frightful debasement, anguish, and outrage is inflicted on us.

We have no access to courts of justice, no voice in the election of rulers, no agency in making the laws,—not even the miserable remnant of liberty, in choosing the despot who may have absolute power over us.

We are hopelessly consigned to that condition most revolting and loathsome

CAN SLAVES RIGHTFULLY RESIST AND FIGHT?

to one in whom the least vestige of manly or womanly feeling is left,—that of absolute slavery.

The laws treat us not as human beings, but "as *chattels personal*, to all intents, constructions, and purposes whatsoever."

Great numbers of our people, in, addition to all these enormities, endure unutterable bodily sufferings, from the cruelty and torturing punishments inflicted on us.

I do not assert that three millions of people, suffering such intolerable wrongs and outrages, ought to throttle their oppressors, and kill fifty thousand of them. I only say, that *if* it was right to do so in 1776, it is also right to do the same in 1852. *If* the light oppressions which the men of the last century endured justified war and bloodshed, then oppressions ten thousand times worse, would surely justify revolt and blood. *If* the colonists might rightfully refuse to "remain in the calling wherein they were called," as subjects of the English government, then slaves may rightfully refuse to continue in the calling wherein they were called. *If* three millions of men might lawfully disregard the text, "honor the king," on the ground that the king oppressed them; then three millions of men may lawfully disregard the text, "servants, obey your masters," on the ground that those masters grievously oppress them. *If* the *prospect of success* justified the war of 1776, then as soon as three millions of slaves feel able and determined to vindicate their rights, they may justly demand them at the point of the sword; and any black Washington who shall lead his countrymen to victory and liberty, even through carnage, will merit our veneration. *If* "liberty or death" was a noble and Christian war-cry in 1776 for the oppressed, then it would be noble and Christian-like for the oppressed men of 1852 practically to adopt the same.

If these inferences appear startling and even horrible, why do they so appear? Is there any reason except that inveterate prejudice, which applies very different principles to the colored man and to the white man? If three millions of white men were in slavery in Algiers now, should we not urge them, as soon as there was hope of success, to imitate the men of 1776, rise and fight for liberty? Therefore, until we are prepared to condemn our ancestors as guilty rebels, and abhor their insurrection as a wicked resistance to the ordinance of God, can we blame *any class* of people for successful revolt against an oppressive government?

Let this further question be pondered. Who were to blame for the destruction of one hundred thousand lives in the war of 1776? The oppressors, or the oppressed? The men who fought for liberty, or the men who would not let them have it without fighting? Who then would be responsible for the death of one hundred thousand men, if the oppressed men of 1852 should kill so many, in fighting for liberty?

If the reader is shocked by such inquiries and inferences, and as directly and intentionally designed to encourage servile insurrection and civil war, he may be assured that my aim is entirely different. It is my wish, to secure timely precautions against danger. For we are to remember, that our slave and colored population is advancing with the same gigantic rate of increase characteristic of our country. In twenty-five years, we shall have six millions of slaves; in fifty years, twelve millions; in seventy-five years, twenty-four millions. Can any one dream of the possibility of retaining twenty-four millions, or twelve millions, of human beings in slavery? Long before that number is reached, will not vast multitudes of them learn the simple lessons of liberty and right, which our books, orations, and politicians inculcate day by day? Will there not arise among them men of courage, genius, enthusiasm, who will, at all hazards, lead them on to that glorious liberty which we have taught them is cheaply purchased at any peril, or war, or bloodshed? When that day comes, as sure it must, will there not be horrors such as civil war has never yet produced? Is it not wise, then, to begin measures for averting so fearful a catastrophe? Is it not madness to slumber over such a frightful future? Should not the talent and energies of the country be directed to the momentous inquiry, How can slavery *now* be peacefully and rightfully removed? Does not every attempt to hush agitation, and insist on the finality of anti-slavery measures, make more sure the awful fact that slavery is to work out its own emancipation in fighting and blood?

Rev. Geo. W. Perkins

DEATH IN LIFE.

SUPPOSED INSCRIPTION UPON THE SEPULCHRE OF A NEGRO SLAVE, WHO, FOR SOME IMAGINED CRIME, HAD BEEN IMMURED HALF A CENTURY IN A DUNGEON.

Ope, jealous portal! ope thy cavern womb,
Thy pris'ner will not flee its close embrace;
He lived and moved too long within a tomb,
Beyond its narrow bounds to dream of space.

To eat his crust and muse, unvarying lot!
Thus, like his beard, his life slow length'ning grew;
So long shut out, the world the wretch forgot,
His cell his universe,—'twas all he knew.

For Memory soon with loving pinions wheeled
In circles narrowing each successive flight;
Her sickly wings at length enfeebled yield,
Too weak to scale the walls that bound his sight.

But Hope sat with him once, and cheered his day;
And raised his limbs, and kept his lamp alight;
Scared by his groans, at length she fled away;
And left him lone,—to spend one endless night.

What change to him, then, is the vault below,
From that where late the captive was confined?
But this,—a worm *here* eats his BODY now;
Whilst *there* it gnawed his slow decaying MIND.

E. Button,

Ebenezer Button..

London, 1852.

TRUE REFORM.

I HAVE received your appeal, my friends, and am not sorry to find myself remembered by you. Every moment of the ages is pregnant with the fate of humanity, but we are inclined to imagine that in which we live to have a peculiar significance. At this hour, it seems to us as if the great balance of justice swayed to and fro, in most disheartening uncertainty; but this moment, like all others, lies in the hollow of God's hand, and his infinite love will not fail to justify to men and angels its terrible discipline.

I have departed on this occasion from the plan of action once laid down to myself. I have not presented you in these pages with the revolting facts of slavery; for to deal with the subject at this moment in a fitting manner, demands a prudence and tact not likely to be possessed by one absent from the scene of action, and ignorant of the passing moment. I wish to convey to you the assurance of my deep sympathy in all Christ-like opposition to sin; my deep sorrow for every loss of manly self-control, and failure of faith in God, among reformers; my conviction that the Constitution of the United States, in so far as it is not in harmony with the law of God, can be no sure foundation for the law of man; that until it gives place to a higher ground of union, or until the nation consent to give it a higher interpretation, it will depress the national industry, corrupt the national morals, and palsy the national strength. It is my firm faith, that man owes his first allegiance to God, and that it is the duty of every citizen who disobeys the law of a land, to bear its penalties with a patience and firmness which shall show him adequate to the hour, and neither unwilling nor unfit to complete the sacrifice he has begun. Above all, O my friends! I pray that God may fill the hearts of the reformers in this cause, with the deepest devotion to His absolute truth, the truest perception of the humility of Christ; that He may show them how, as its exigencies press, they must not only be men full of anti-slavery zeal, but filled with Divine prudence, sincere desirers of that peace which is founded on purity,—possessors of that temperance which is its own best pledge. In the consciousness of the martyrdom of the affections, which his position involves, the reformer feels oftentimes secure of his eternal compensation. But I have wondered, of late, whether martyrdom may not be as dangerous to his spiritual life as worldly renown, or pecuniary prosperity.

Stretched upon the rack, I may still be puffed up with pride, or an unhealthy spirit of self-dependence; and sacrificing my last copper on the altar of a great truth, I may still refuse to offer there my personal vanity, my wilful self-esteem, or my bitterness of temper.

Let us be willing, O my friends! to lay these also at the feet of Christ.

Mrs Caroline W. Healey Dall.

Toronto, Canada, July 22, 1852.

HOW LONG?

How long, O gracious God! how long,
Shall power lord it over right?
The feeble, trampled by the strong,
Remain in slavery's gloomy night?
In every region of the earth,
Oppression rules with iron power;
And every man of sterling worth,
Whose soul disdains to cringe or cower
Beneath a haughty tyrant's nod,
And, supplicating, kiss the rod
That, wielded by oppression's might,
Smites to the earth his dearest right,—
The right to speak, and think, and feel,
And spread his uttered thoughts abroad,
To labor for the common weal,
Responsible to none but God,—
Is threatened with the dungeon's gloom,
The felon's cell, the traitor's doom,
And treacherous politicians league
With hireling priests, to crush and ban
All who expose their vile intrigue,
And vindicate the rights of man.
How long shall Afric' raise to thee
Her fettered hand, O Lord! in vain,
And plead in fearful agony
For vengeance for her children slain?
I see the Gambia's swelling flood,
And Niger's darkly rolling wave,
Bear on their bosoms, stained with blood,
The bound and lacerated slave;
While numerous tribes spread near and far,
Fierce, devastating, barbarous war,
Earth's fairest scenes in ruin laid,
To furnish victims for that trade,
Which breeds on earth such deeds of shame,
As fiends might blush to hear or name.
I see where Danube's waters roll,

HOW LONG?

And where the Magyar vainly strove,
With valiant arm and faithful soul,
In battle for the land he loved, —
A perjured tyrant's legions tread
The ground where Freedom's heroes bled,
And still the voice of those who feel
Their country's wrongs, with Austrian steel.
I see the "Rugged Russian Bear,"
Lead forth his slavish hordes, to war
Upon the right of every State
Its own affairs to regulate;
To help each despot bind the chain
Upon the people's rights again,
And crush beneath his ponderous paw
All constitutions, rights, and law.
I see in France, — O burning shame! —
The shadow of a mighty name,
Wielding the power her patriot bands
Had boldly wrenched from kingly hands,
With more despotic pride of sway
Than ever monarch dared display.
The Fisher, too, whose world-wide nets
Are spread to snare the souls of men,
By foreign tyrants' bayonets
Established on his throne again,
Blesses the swords still reeking red
With the best blood his country bore,
And prays for blessings on the head
Of him who wades through Roman gore.
The same unholy sacrifice
Where'er I turn bursts on mine eyes,
Of princely pomp, and priestly pride,
The people trampled in the dust,
Their dearest, holiest rights denied,
Their hopes destroyed, their spirit crushed:
But when I turn the land to view,
Which claims, par excellence, to be
The refuge of the brave and true,
The strongest bulwark of the free,
The grand asylum for the poor
And trodden down of every land,
Where they may rest in peace, secure,
Nor fear the oppressor's iron hand, —
Worse scenes of rapine, lust, and shame,
Than e'er disgraced the Russian name,
Worse than the Austrian ever saw,

Are sanctioned here as righteous law.
Here might the Austrian butcher[13] make
Progress in shameful cruelty,
Where women-whippers proudly take
The meed and praise of chivalry.
Here might the cunning Jesuit learn,
Though skilled in subtle sophistry,
And trained to persevere in stern
Unsympathizing cruelty,
And call that good, which, right or wrong,
Will tend to make his order strong:
He here might learn from those who stand
High in the gospel ministry,
The very magnates of the land
In evangelic piety,
That conscience must not only bend
To everything the church decrees,
But it must also condescend,
When drunken politicians please
To place their own inhuman acts
Above the "higher law" of God,
And on the hunted victim's tracks
Cheer the malignant fiends of blood,
To help the man-thief bind the chain
Upon his Christian brother's limb,
And bear to slavery's hell again
The bound and suffering child of Him
Who died upon the cross, to save
Alike, the master and the slave.
While all the oppressed from every land
Are welcomed here with open hand,
And fulsome praises rend the heaven
For those who have the fetters riven
Of European tyranny,
And bravely struck for liberty;
And while from thirty thousand fanes
Mock prayers go up, and hymns are sung,
Three million drag their clanking chains,
"Unwept, unhonored, and unsung;"
Doomed to a state of slavery,
Compared with which the darkest night
Of European tyranny,
Seems brilliant as the noonday light.
While politicians void of shame,
Cry this is law and liberty,

---
[13] Haynau.

HOW LONG?

The clergy lend the awful name
And sanction of the Deity,
To help sustain the monstrous wrong,
And crush the weak beneath the strong.
Lord, thou hast said the tyrant's ear
Shall not be always closed to thee,
But that thou wilt in wrath appear,
And set the trembling captive free.
And even now dark omens rise
To those who either see or hear,
And gather o'er the darkening skies
The threatening signs of fate and fear;
Not like the plagues which Egypt saw,
When rising in an evil hour,
A rebel 'gainst the "higher law,"
And glorying in her mighty power,—
Saw blasting fire, and blighting hail,
Sweep o'er her rich and fertile vale,
And heard on every rising gale
Ascend the bitter mourning wail;
And blighted herd, and blasted plain,
Through all the land the first-born slain,
Her priests and magi made to cower
In witness of a higher power,
And darkness like a sable pall
Shrouding the land in deepest gloom,
Sent sadly through the minds of all,
Forebodings of approaching doom.
What though no real shower of fire
Spreads o'er this land its withering blight,
Denouncing wide Jehovah's ire
Like that which palsied Egypt's might;
And though no literal darkness spreads
Upon the land its sable gloom,
And seems to fling around our heads
The awful terrors of the tomb;
Yet to the eye of him who reads
The fate of nations past and gone,
And marks with care the wrongful deeds
By which their power was overthrown,—
Worse plagues than Egypt ever felt
Are seen wide-spreading through the land,
Announcing that the heinous guilt
On which the nation proudly stands,
Has risen to Jehovah's throne,
And kindled his Almighty ire,

And broadcast through the land has sown
The seeds of a devouring fire;
Blasting with foul pestiferous breath,
The fountain springs of moral life,
And planting deep the seeds of death,
And future germs of deadly strife;
And moral darkness spreads its gloom
Over the land in every part,
And buries in a living tomb
Each generous prompting of the heart.
Vice in its darkest, deadliest stains,
Here walks with brazen front abroad,
And foul corruption proudly reigns
Triumphant in the church of God,
And sinks so low the Christian name,
In foul degrading vice and shame,
That Moslem, Heathen, Atheist, Jew,
And men of every faith and creed,
To their professions far more true,
More liberal both in word and deed,
May well reject with loathing scorn
The doctrines taught by those who sell
Their brethren in the Saviour born,
Down into slavery's hateful hell;
And with the price of Christian blood
Build temples to the Christian's God,
And offer up as sacrifice,
And incense to the God of heaven,
The mourning wail, and bitter cries,
Of mothers from their children riven;
Of virgin purity profaned
To sate some brutal ruffian's lust,
Millions of godlike minds ordained
To grovel ever in the dust,
Shut out by Christian power and might
From every ray of Christian light.
How long, O Lord! shall such vile deeds
Be acted in thy holy name,
And senseless bigots o'er their creeds
Fill the whole world with war and flame?
How long shall ruthless tyrants claim
Thy sanction to their bloody laws,
And throw the mantle of thy name
Around their foul, unhallowed cause?
How long shall all the people bow
As vassals of the favored few,

HOW LONG?

And shame the pride of manhood's brow, —
Give what to God alone is due,
Homage, to wealth, and rank, and power,
Vain shadows of a passing hour?
Oh for a pen of living fire,
A tongue of flame, an arm of steel!
To rouse the people's slumbering ire,
And teach the tyrants' hearts to feel.
O Lord! in vengeance now appear,
And guide the battles for the right,
The spirits of the fainting cheer,
And nerve the patriot's arm with might;
Till slavery, banished from the world,
And tyrants from their power hurled,
And all mankind from bondage free,
Exult in glorious liberty!

J. M. Whitfield.

LETTER FROM WILSON ARMISTEAD TO THE SECRETARY OF THE SOCIETY.

LEEDS, 7TH MO. 22, 1852.

MY DEAR FRIEND:—

In responding to thy welcome communication, I may say that I rejoice in the cause of the interruption of our correspondence, so far as it concerns thyself; thy time and talents being so increasingly occupied, in union with other of humanity's advocates, in assisting to overturn the monster iniquity of our age, that crowning crime of Christendom,—*negro slavery!*

Go on in this good work! and may God's blessing abundantly attend, till the eternal overthrow be effected of a system so fraught with every evil; so abhorrent to the rights of nature, and so contrary to the spirit of the Gospel;—till the galling chain be broken off the necks of America's three million slaves; till its victims be raised from the profoundest depths of ignorance and woe, to which they are now degraded.

'Tis a marvel to me, that a system like that of negro slavery, which admits of such atrocities, can be tolerated for a single hour! Ought not every one who has a spark of humanity, to say nothing of Christianity, in his bosom,—ought not all the sound part of every community in which slavery exists to rise up *en masse*, and declare that, this abomination shall exist no longer?

Who gave to any man the right to enslave his fellow man? Can any enactment of human legislators so far sanction robbery, as lawfully to make one man the property of another? Has God poured the tide of life through the African's breast, and animated it with a portion of his own Divine spirit, and at the same time deprived him of all natural affections, that *he* alone is to be struck off the list of rational beings, and placed on a level with the brute? Is his flesh marble, and his sinews iron, or his immortal spirit of a class condemned, without hope, to penal suffering, that he is called upon to endure incessant toil, and to be subjected to degradation, bodily and mental, such as no other portion of the family of Adam have ever been destined to endure, without the vengeance of Heaven being signally displayed upon the oppressors? Does the African mother feel less love to her offspring than the white woman? or the African husband regard with less tenderness the wife of his bosom? Is his heart dead to the ties of kindred,—his nature so brutalized, that the sacred associations of home and country awaken no emotions in his breast?

History unanswerably demonstrates that the negro does feel, keenly feel, the wrongs inflicted upon him by his unrighteous enslavers, and that his mind, barren as it has been rendered by hard usage, and desolated with misery, is not unwatered by the pure and gentle streams of natural affection. Yet the lordly oppressors remain unmoved by the sad condition of the negro, contemplate with indifference his bodily and mental sufferings, and still dare to postpone to an indefinite period the termination of his oppression and of their own guilt.

But thanks be to God! there *is* some counteracting influence to this feeling, and that it is on the advance. The night has been long and dark,—already the horizon brightens; the day of freedom dawns.

Go on, then, my friend; I say, go on! in the good cause thou hast espoused. Labor, and faint not. "Whatsoever thy hand findeth to do, do it with all thy might." My kind regards to Frederick Douglass; may he, and all others also, be strengthened and encouraged to labor in the great work of human freedom; that so, by gradual increase, like the mighty surge, they may become strong enough to overpower and drown the oppressor, and be enabled to devise and execute measures of mercy and justice, which may avert the judgments of the Almighty from their guilty land. For surely some signal display of Divine displeasure must await America, unless she repent, and undo the heavy burdens of her THREE MILLION SLAVES.

Are not the signs of the times calculated to remind us forcibly of this language of Isaiah, "Behold, the Lord cometh out of his place to punish the inhabitants of the earth for their iniquity; the earth also shall disclose her blood, and no more cover her slain." Do we not hear already

> "— —the wheels of an avenging God,
> Groan heavily along the distant road?"

Assuredly, he comes to judge the earth. "Who shall abide the day of his coming; who shall stand when he appeareth?"

Thy Friend, very truly,

Wilson Armistead

IMPROMPTU STANZAS,

SUGGESTED BY THE WORKING OF THE FUGITIVE SLAVE ACT, AS ILLUSTRATED IN THE CASE OF REV. DOCTOR PENNINGTON.

BY THE WORK-SHOP BARD.

Bring out the handcuffs, clank the rusted gyves;
Rain down your curses on the doomed race;
Hang out a terror that shall haunt their lives,
In every place.

Unloose the bloodhounds from oppression's den;
Arm every brigand in the name of law,
And triple shield of pulpit, press, and pen,
Around them draw.

Ho! politicians, orators, divines!
Ho! cotton-mongers of the North and South!
Strike now for slavery, or our Union's shrines
Are gone forsooth!
Down from their glory into chaos hurled,
Your thirty States in shivered fragments go,
Like the seared leaves by autumn tempests whirled
To depths below.

Closed be each ear, let every tongue be dumb;
Nor one sad pitying tear o'er man be shed,
Though fainting at your threshold he should come,
And ask for bread.

Though woman, fleeing from the cruel grip
Of foul oppression, scarred and stained with blood,
Where from the severed veins the driver's whip
Hath drank its flood.

Though helpless childhood ask—O pitying Heaven!—
The merest crumb which falls upon the floor,
Tho' faint and famished, bread must not be given,
Bolt fast the door.

And must it be, thou just and holy God!
That in our midst thy peeled and stricken poor

IMPROMPTU STANZAS, 37

Shall kneel and plead amid their tears and blood,
For evermore?

Shall those whom thou hast sent baptized from heaven,
To preach the Gospel the wide world around,
To teach the erring they may be forgiven,
Be seized and bound?

Placed on the auction-block, with chattels sold,
Driven like beasts of burden day by day,
The flock be scattered from the shepherd's fold,
The spoiler's prey?

How long—thy people cry—O Lord, how long!
Shall not thine arm "shake down the bolted fire!"
Can deeds like these of God-defying wrongs,
Escape His ire?

Must judgments,—such as swept with fearful tread
O'er Egypt when she made thy people slaves,
Where thy hand strewed with their unburied dead
The Red Sea waves?

Must fire and hail from heaven upon us fall,
Our first-born perish 'neath the Avenger's brand,
And sevenfold darkness, like a funeral pall
O'erspread the land?

We kneel before thy footstool, gracious God,
Spare thou our nation, in thy mercy spare;
We perish quickly 'neath thy lifted rod
And arm made bare.

J. M. Eells.

J. M. Eells.

WEST TROY, MARCH, 1851.

JOHN MURRAY (OF GLASGOW).

ABOUT a year ago, the newspapers announced the death of Mr. John Murray, for many years the secretary of the Glasgow Emancipation Society, and I would do violence to truth and humanity whose servant and soldier he was, should I neglect to pen a few recollections of that most earnest and efficient man.

He was related to the ancient and honorable family of the Oswalds of Sheildhall, and received that excellent educational and religious training which is given to the children of the middle and higher classes in Scotland. At the age of twenty-two or three, in consequence of an attack of pulmonary hemorrhage, he sailed for the West Indies and found employment at his trade, house-building, in St. Kitts. Very soon, however, he found other matters to engage, and almost engross his attention and labors; in conjunction with an uncle of George Stephen of London, and a Dr. Hamilton, resident in St. Kitts, he did manly and successful fight in behalf of the wronged and bleeding slave.

After a residence in that island of some years, during which he obtained a thorough knowledge of the workings of slavery, he returned to Glasgow, poor in pocket, but rich in abolitionism. Soon after his return, he was united in marriage to Miss Anna — —, a lady whose perfect harmony in sentiment, softened by feminine delicacy, made a happy anti-slavery home for the zealous and ardent abolitionism of John Murray. It was a union of hearts attached in early youth, and which had remained "leal" during a long separation.

Shortly after marriage, he commenced business as a *spirit-dealer*, then and now a most reputable calling in the opinion of the good citizens of Glasgow. Temperate himself, his calling gradually became unpleasant to him. At first he refused to sell spirits to any person partly inebriated; then he reasoned himself into a total abandonment of the death-dealing traffic. With no other business prospect before him, prevented by his long difficulty from working at his trade, with a young wife and child dependent on him, he suddenly locked up his spirit-cellar and never more sold rum!

In 1828 or 1829, through the influence of his kinsman, James Oswald, Esq., of Sheildhall, Mr. Murray was appointed surveyor on a part of the Forth and Clyde canal, an office requiring much labor for little pay. His prospects of promotion depended on Mr. Oswald and other members of the Kirk of Scotland. Mr. Murray was a full member of the Tron Church, Glasgow, when, according to law, a minister was appointed there regardless of the choice, and contrary to the wishes of the great majority of its members. In consequence of this appointment, and again unmindful of personal advancement, John Murray shook the dust from his sandals and quit at once and forever the Tron Church and the Kirk of Scotland.

About the same time the Glasgow Emancipation Society was formed or re-organized, on the doctrine of immediate emancipation so splendidly announced by a secession minister of Edinburgh. The secretaries of this association were John Murray the surveyor, and William Smead, of the Gallowgate, grocer; the last a Friend. These two were the head and front, the thinking and the locomotive power of this well known association which did notable fight, if not the principal labor, in effecting emancipation in the British West Indies, and in assaulting American slavery.

And, twenty odd years ago, it was no trifling matter to do anti-slavery work in Glasgow, the very names of whose stateliest streets proclaimed that they were built by money wrung out of the blood and sweat of the negroes of Jamaica, St. Vincents, etc. The whole of the retired wealth, nearly all the active business influence, the weight of the Established Church, the rank and fashion of Glasgow, and though last not least, the keen wit of the poet Motherwell,[14] and the great statistical learning and industry of M'Queen were arrayed on the side of the slave-holder. Sugar and cotton and rum were lords of the ascendant! Yet the poor surveyor and the humble grocer fought on; nor did they fight alone; the silvery voice and keen acumen of Ralph Wardlaw, the earnest and powerful Hugh Heugh, the inexorable logic and burning sarcasm of swarthy Wully Anderson, and the princely munificence of James Johnston, combined to awaken the people to the enormity of slavery. And the Voluntary Church movement, and the fight for the Reform Bill aroused a varied eloquence in the orators who plead for, and a kindling enthusiasm in the people who were struggling on the liberal side of all these questions; for the people, battling for their own rights, had heart room to hear the prayer for the rights of others more deeply oppressed. Thus ever will liberty be expansive and expanding in the direction of human brotherhood.

Then KNIBB came along with his fiery eloquence, which swept over and warmed the hearts of the people with indignation at the dishonor done religion in the martyrdom of the missionary Smith; and then the grand scene in the British emancipation drama, the overthrow of Bostwick by George Thompson, and the monster petitions and the reluctant assent of the ministry and the passage of the bill.

Those were stirring times in Glasgow, and it did one's heart good to see John Murray in their midst. The arrangements for nearly all those movements originated with, and were carried out by him; he never made a speech of one minute long, yet he most effectively arranged all the speaking, drew up all the resolutions and reports and addresses; and most of the movements in England, the pressure upon the ministry, and the advocacy in Parliament were the result of his wide and laborious correspondence. He used more than one ream of paper for manuscripts upon the great cause which he seemed born to carry out successfully. In addition to his other correspondence, nearly every issue of two of the Glasgow tri-weekly papers contained able articles from his pen in reply to the elaborate defence of

[14] Editor of the Glasgow Courier. Poor Motherwell! I have it from a mutual friend that he sympathized *with* the cause of Freedom, while paid to write against it.

slavery carried on in the Glasgow Courier by Mr. M'Queen. And yet this man, doing this mighty work, was so entirely unobtrusive, so quiet in his labors, that few beyond the committee knew him other than the silent secretary of the Glasgow Emancipation Society. And I shall not soon forget the perfect consternation with which he heard a vote of thanks tendered him by resolution at an annual meeting of the society.

In 1835 or 1836, Mr. Murray was promoted to the office of collector at Bowling Bay, for the company he had so long and faithfully served. And many an anti-slavery wayfarer can testify to the warm welcome and genial hospitality of the snug little stone building so beautifully packed on the Clyde entrance of the Forth and Clyde canal. A charming family, consisting of a devoted wife, two most promising boys, and a retiring, sweet tempered girl, made happy the declining years of this great friend of the slave, and earnest pioneer in many reforms. Freedom for Ireland, the Peace Question, Radical Reform, a Free Church, and Total Abstinence, were questions to all of which Mr. Murray devoted his pen and his purse. His soul received and advocated whatever looked towards human progress.

In person, Mr. Murray was tall and gaunt, and would strongly remind one of Henry Clay. About a mile from Bowling Bay, within the enclosure that surrounds the Relief Church, in a sweet quiet spot, the green turf now covers what remains of the once active frame of John Murray; and as, with moistened cheek, I fling this pebble upon his cairn, I cannot help thinking how much more has been done for the cause of human progress by this faithful servant to his own convictions of the truth, than by the nation-wept sage of Ashland.

James M'Cune Smith

James M'Cune Smith

NEW YORK, SEPT. 25, 1852.

POWER OF AMERICAN EXAMPLE.

AT the last anniversary of the American Home Missionary Society, Rev. John P. Gulliver made an eloquent address on the duty of bringing the American people under the full influence of Christian principle, in an argument drawn from the bearings of our national example on the people of other lands. *Christianity*, he said, *alone can make the nations free*. We fully believe in this sentiment. In answer to the question, *How is Christianity to effect this result?*—Mr. Gulliver's answer was: AMERICA IS TO BE THE AGENT.

Other nations, he thought, might do much in working out this great result; but the chief hopes of the friends of freedom, he suggested, are centered upon this country. The world needs *an example*; and he pointed to what the example of this nation has already done, imperfect as it is. "It is doing, at this moment, more to change the political condition of man than all the armies and navies,—than all the diplomacy and king-craft of the world." If it be so, if, as the speaker declared, "the battle of the world's freedom is to be fought on our own soil," it would be interesting to look at the obstacles in the way. The United States must present a very different example from that exhibited the last twenty-five years, and now exhibited, before this country will be the agent of Christianity in evangelizing the world. Think of three millions of our countrymen in chains! Think of the large numbers held by ministers of the gospel and members of churches! Think of the countenance given to slave-holders by our ecclesiastical assemblies, by Northern preachers, by Christian lawyers, merchants, and mechanics! Think of the platforms, adopted by the two leading political parties of the country, composed partly of religious men! Think of the dumbness of those that minister at the altar, in view of the great national iniquity, and then consider the effects of *such an example* upon other nations, Christian and Heathen!

Dr. Hawes is stated to have said at the last annual meeting of the A. B. C. F. M., that Dr. John H. Rice said, in his hearing, more than twenty years ago: "I do not believe the Lord will suffer the existing type or character of the Christian world to be impressed on the heathen." We also heard the remark, and believe that Dr. Rice, in alluding to the state of religion in this country, said, "it was so far short of what Christianity required, that sanguine as many were that the United States was speedily to be the agent of the world's conversion, he did not believe, for one, that God would suffer the Christianity of this country, as it then was, to be impressed upon the heathen world." If the character of our religion was thus twenty years ago, what is it now? As a religious people we have been boastful. We have acted as if we thought God could not convert the world without the instrumentality of this country. It is far more probable that the converted heathen will send missionaries to the United States to teach us the first rudiments of Christianity, than that this country, at the present low ebb of religion, will be the agent of converting heathen nations to God.

Dr. Hawes believed "that if the piety of the church were corrected and raised to the standard of Paul, God would soon give to the Son the heathen for his inheritance." No doubt of it. Such piety would do away with chattel slavery, with caste, with slavery platforms, with ungodly rulers, with Indian oppression, with divorcing Christianity from the ballot-box, with heathenism at home. Let us pray for such piety; and that hundreds of such men as RICE and HAWES may lift up their voices like a trumpet, and put forth corresponding action, until the nation shall be regenerated and become fit to enlighten, and, through the grace of God, save a dying world.

Lewis Tappan.

"THE GOSPEL AS A REMEDY FOR SLAVERY."

In one of the leading Congregational papers, a writer, W. C. J., has commenced a series of communications under the above heading. It is well to discuss the subject. The writer says, "There are, it is true, many among our three millions of slaves who are acquainted with the rudiments of religious truth, and are leading lives of sincere piety." Dr. Nelson, a native of a slave State, stated, as the result of experience for many years, that he had never known more than three or four slaves who he had reason to believe were truly and intelligently pious. The Synod of South Carolina and Georgia published to the world, some years since, that the great mass of slaves were heathen, as much so as the heathen of any portion of the globe. What authority W. C. J. has for saying there are, among the three millions of American slaves, "many" who are "leading lives of sincere piety," I do not know. It is probably the mere conjecture of an ardent mind. He qualifies the expression by asking, "What is the type of the religion that too generally appears among the slaves?" And then replies to his own question, "It is sickly and weak, like a plant growing in a cellar, or a cave; a compound of sincere piety with much of superstition and fanaticism." What sort of piety is that?

A sagacious observer has remarked, that there never can be, in our day, intelligent piety where men are not possessed of property, especially where they are mere serfs or slaves. How many American slaves have the piety of "Uncle Tom," we are unable to say. Probably very few. And it must fill the heart of every one who loves the souls of men, with anguish to contemplate the spiritual destitution of the slaves in this country; kept in bondage by the religious and political apathy or acts of professing Christians, of different denominations, in their individual or associated capacity. But to the question: *Is the gospel a remedy for slavery?* We answer, unhesitatingly, not such a gospel as is preached to them; for while it does very little to enlighten either slave or master, it enjoins upon the former passive obedience, and inculcates upon the latter the right and duty of holding their fellow men in bondage. Nor have we much hesitation in avowing it as our belief, that the gospel, as generally preached in the free States, is quite inadequate to put an end to slavery. It does not reach the conscience of the tens of thousands who are, in various ways, connected with slave-holding by relationship, business correspondence, or political or ecclesiastical ties. As proof of this, we need only contemplate the action of the Northern divisions of the political and religious national parties. Slavery is countenanced, strengthened, increased, extended by their connivance or direct agency. The truth is, Christianity, as promulgated by the great mass of the preachers and professors at this day even in the free States, is not a remedy for slavery. It is a lamentable truth, one that might justly occasion in the heart of every true Christian the lamentation of the prophet Jeremiah: "Oh that my head were waters, and mine eyes a fountain of tears, that I might weep, day and night, for the slain of the daughters of my people!" And it is in view of this truth, that the friends of a pure and full gospel have great encouragement to persevere in their work of faith and love. The missionaries connected with the American Missionary Association, at home and abroad, inculcate, fearlessly and persistently, a gospel of freedom, and make no more apology or allowance for slave-holding than for any other sin or crime. Such missionaries should be sustained, their numbers augmented, and prayer ascend for them continually.

Lewis Tappan

LETTER TO THE PRESIDENT OF THE SOCIETY.

Dear Madam:—

Your request to transmit my name, with a short article, for insertion in your contemplated publication, is before me. I have neither time nor words in which to express my unalterable abhorrence of slavery, with all the odious apologies and blasphemous claims of Divine sanction for it, that have been attempted. I regard all attempts, by legislation or otherwise, to give the abominable system "aid and comfort" as involving treason against the government of God, and as insulting the consciences and common sense of men.

Yours truly,

C. G. Finney

C. G. Finney

Oberlin, 24 Sept., 1852.

THE SLAVE'S PRAYER.

The *first effort* of my early life in narrative writing, was in behalf of those who, in even darker days than these, were preëminently those who, on earth, "had no helper."

From this tale is selected these few lines—a song introduced into the story—not because it has any poetic merit, but because to me and perhaps to others, it seems interesting from the above circumstance.

Catharine E. Beecher.

Miss Catharine E. Beecher.

SONG OF PRAISE.

Though man neglects my sighing,
And mocks the bitter tear,
Yet does not God my crying
With kindest pity hear?

And when with fierce heat panting
His hand can be my shade,
And when with weakness fainting
Support my aching head.

And when I felt my cares
For those his love can save,
Will he not hear the prayers
Of the poor negro slave?

Yes, for the poor and needy
He promises to save,
And who is poor and needy
Like the poor negro slave!

THE STRUGGLE.

Ours is a noble cause; nobler even than that of our fathers, inasmuch as it is more exalted to struggle for the freedom of *others*, than for our *own*. The love of right, which is the animating impulse of our movement, is higher even than the love of freedom. But right, freedom, and humanity, all concur in demanding the abolition of slavery.

Charles Sumner

Hon. Charles Sumner

Boston, Oct. 16, 1852.

WORK AND WAIT.

My Friend:—

I have found no moment till the present that I could devote to a compliance with your request, and I am now probably too late. However, let me hastily proffer a few suggestions to opponents of slavery, which I trust may not be found unprofitable. I would say, then:

1. Do not choose to separate and isolate yourselves from the general movement of humanity, save as you may be constrained to oppose certain eddies of that movement. Had Wilberforce, Clarkson, and their associate pioneers in the cause of British abolition, seen fit to cut themselves loose from all preëxisting sects and parties, and for a special anti-slavery church and party, I think the triumph of their cause would have been still unattained.

2. Do not refuse to do a little good because you would much prefer to do a greater which is now unattainable. The earth revolves in her vast orbit gradually; and he who has done whatever good he can, need not reproach himself for his inability to do more.

3. Be foremost in every good work that the community around you *will* appreciate,—not *because* they will appreciate it, but because their appreciation and sympathy will enable you to do good in other spheres, and do it more effectually.

4. Be preëminent in your consideration and regard for the rights and wrongs of labor in your own circle, even the rudest and humblest. An abolitionist who hires his linen made up at the lowest market rate, and pays his wash-woman in proportion, will do little good to the anti-slavery or any other philanthrophic cause. The man of liberal culture and generous heart who unostentatiously tries to elevate the most depressed to his own level, is doing a good work against slavery, however unconsciously.

5. Have faith, with a divine patience; man is privileged to labor for a good cause, but the glory of its success must redound to his Maker. Next to a great defeat, the most fatal event for slavery would be a great triumph. Doubtless, the bolts are now forging in some celestial armory destined to strike the shackles from the limbs of the bondman, and cleanse the land from the foulest and blackest iniquity ever organized and legalized in the christian world. The shout of deliverance may come when it is least expected,—nay, the very means employed to render its coming impossible, will probably secure and hasten it. For that and every other needed reform, let the humane and hopeful strive, not despairing in the densest midnight, and realizing that the darkest hour is often that preceding the dawn. Let

them, squandering no opportunity, and sacrificing no principle,

"Learn to labor, and to wait."

Horace Greeley

THE GREAT EMANCIPATION.

Beautiful and happy will this world be, when slavery and every other form of oppression shall have ceased. But this change can be produced only by the religion of Jesus Christ. Reliance on any other power to overthrow slavery, or restore to order and happiness this sin-crazed and sin-ruined world, will be vain.

Gerrit Smith

Peterboro', Sept. 22, 1852.

ODE

Sung at the celebration of the First Anniversary of the kidnapping, at Boston, of Thomas Sims, a fugitive slave:—the kidnapping done under the forms of law, and by its officers, 12 June 1851. The deed *celebrated* at the Melodeon, Boston, 12 June 1852.

BY REV. JOHN PIERPONT.

Souls of the patriot dead,
On Bunker's height who bled!
The pile, that stands
On your long-buried bones,—
Those monumental stones,—
Should not suppress the groans,
This day demands.

For Freedom there ye stood;
There gave the earth your blood;
There found your graves;
That men of every clime,
Faith, color, tongue, and time,
Might, through your death sublime,
Never be slaves.

LIBERTY

Over your bed, so low,
Heard ye not, long ago,
A voice of power[15]
Proclaim to earth and sea,
That, where ye sleep, should be
A home for Liberty,
Till Time's last hour?

---

[15] Daniel Webster's oration, at the laying the corner-stone of Bunker Hill Monument, 17 June 1825.

ODE

Hear ye the chains of slaves,
Now clanking round your graves?
Hear ye the sound
Of that same voice, that calls

From out our Senate halls,[16]
"Hunt down those fleeing thralls,
With horse and hound!"

That voice your sons hath swayed!
'Tis heard, and is obeyed!
This gloomy day
Tells you of ermine stained,
Of Justice' name profaned,
Of a poor bondman, chained
And borne away!

Over Virginia's Springs,
Her eagles spread their wings,
Her Blue Ridge towers:—

That voice,[17]—once heard with awe,—
Now asks,—"Who ever saw,
Up there, a higher law
Than this of ours?"

Must *we* obey that voice?
When God, or man's the choice,
Must we postpone
HIM, who from Sinai spoke?
Must we wear slavery's yoke?
Bear of her lash the stroke,
And prop her throne?

Lashed with her hounds, must we
Run down the poor, who flee
From Slavery's hell?
Great God! when we *do* this,
Exclude us from thy bliss;
At us let angels hiss,
From heaven that fell!

Rev. John Pierpont

---

[16] Daniel Webster's speech in the Senate of the U. S. 7 March 1850.
[17] Daniel Webster's speech at the Capron Springs, Virginia, 1851.

PASSAGES IN THE LIFE OF A SLAVE WOMAN.

BY ANNIE PARKER.

"The slaves at Oak Grove did not mourn for poor Elsie when she died," said aunt Phillis, continuing her narrative. "She was never a favorite, and from the time her beauty attracted the notice of the young master, and he began to pet her, she grew prouder and prouder, and treated the other slaves as if she were their mistress, rather than their equal. They hated her for her influence over the master, and she knew it, and that made matters worse between them.

"When she died in giving birth to her second child, her little boy and I were the only ones who felt any sorrow. The master had grown tired of her, though he had once been very fond of her. Besides, he was at this time making arrangements for his marriage with a beautiful Northern lady, so that whatever he might have felt, nobody knew anything about it.

"Elsie was my younger sister. I loved her dearly, and had been almost as proud as she was of her remarkable beauty. Her little boy was very fond of his mother, and she doated upon him. He mourned and mourned for her, after her death, till I almost thought he would die too. He was a beautiful boy, and at that time looked very much like his father, which was probably the reason why the master sold him, before he brought his bride to Oak Grove.

"It was very hard for me to part with poor Elsie's little boy. But the master chose to sell him, and my tears availed nothing. Zilpha, Elsie's infant, was given me to take care of when her mother died, and with that I was obliged to be content.

"Marion Lee, the young mistress, was very beautiful, but as different from poor Elsie as light from darkness. She had deep blue eyes, with long silken lashes, and a profusion of soft brown hair. She always made me think of a half-blown rosebud, she was so delicate and fair. She proved a kind and gentle mistress. All the slaves loved her, as well they might, for she did everything in her power to make them comfortable and happy.

"When she came to Oak Grove, she chose me to be her waiting-maid. Zilpha and I occupied a large pleasant room next to her dressing-room.

"She made a great pet of Zilpha. No one ever told her that she was her husband's child. No one would have dared to tell her, even if she had not been too much beloved, for any one to be willing to grieve her, as the knowledge of this fact must have done.

"In due time she, too, had a little girl, beautiful like herself. Zilpha was delighted with the baby. She never wearied of kissing its tiny hands, and talking to it in her sweet coaxing tones. Mrs. Lee said Zilpha should be Ida's little maid. The children, accordingly, grew up together, and when they were old enough to be taught from books, everything that Ida learned, Zilpha learned also.

"When Zilpha was seventeen, she was more beautiful than her mother had ever been, and she was as gentle and loving as Elsie had been passionate and proud. There was a beautiful, pleading look in her large dark eyes, when she lifted the long lashes so that you could see into their clear depths. She was graceful as a young fawn, and playful as a kitten, and she had read and studied so many books, that *I* thought she knew almost as much as the master himself.

"Mr. Minturn lived at Lilybank, the estate joining Oak Grove. He was an old friend of Mr. Lee, and the families were very intimate. About this time a relative of Mrs. Minturn died at the far South, and left her a large number of slaves. I don't know how they were *all* disposed of, but one of the number, a very handsome young man, named Jerry, was brought to Lilybank, and became Mr. Minturn's coachman. He was considered a great prize, for he had a large muscular frame, and was capable of enduring a great amount of bodily fatigue. He was, also, for a slave, very intelligent, and from being at first merely the coachman, he soon became the confidential servant of his master.

"Owing to the intimacy between the heads of the two families, the young people of both were much together. Ida often spent whole days at Lilybank, and as Zilpha always accompanied her, she had ample opportunity to become acquainted with the new man Jerry.

"It so happened that I, being more closely confined by my duties at home, had never seen Jerry, when in the summer following his coming to Lilybank, Mrs. Lee went to visit her friends at the North, and took me with her. Ida and Zilpha remained at home. We were gone three months. A few days after our return, Zilpha told me that she was soon to be married to Jerry. The poor child was very happy. She had evidently given him her whole heart. We talked long that day, for I wanted to know how it had been brought about, and she told me all, with the simplicity and artlessness of a child. They had felt great anxiety lest their masters should oppose the marriage. But that fear was removed. Mr. Lee had himself proposed it, and Mr. Minturn gladly consented. I rejoiced to see my darling so happy, and felt truly thankful to God that the warm love of her heart had not been blighted.

"That same evening Jerry came to see Zilpha. She called me immediately, for I had never seen him, and she wished us to meet. The moment I looked upon his face, I knew he was my poor Elsie's son. I grew sick and faint, and thought I should have fallen.

"Zilpha made me sit down, and brought me a glass of water, wondering all the time, poor thing, what had made me ill so suddenly. I soon recovered sufficiently to remember that I must not betray the cause of my agitation. I did not speak much, but watched Jerry's face as closely as I could, without arresting their attention. Every moment strengthened the conviction that my suspicion was correct.

There was the same proud look that Elsie had, the same flashing eye, and slightly curled lip, and when he carelessly brushed back the hair from his forehead, I saw a scar upon it, which I knew was caused by a fall but a little while before his mother died. O God! I thought, what will become of my darling child!

"I soon left the room, on the pretence that my mistress wanted me, but really that I might shut myself into my own room and think. I did not close my eyes that night, and when the morning dawned, I was as far as ever from knowing what I ought to do. At last I resolved to see the master as early as I could, and tell him all.

"After breakfast I went to the library to fetch a book for my mistress, and found the master there. He was reading, but looked up as I entered, and said kindly, 'What do you wish for, Phillis?' I named the book my mistress wanted. He told me where it was. I took it from the shelf, and stood with it in my hand. The opportunity which I desired had come, but I trembled from head to foot, and had no power to speak. I don't know how I ever found words to tell him that Jerry was his own child. I tried, afterwards, to remember what I said, but I could not recall a word. He turned deadly pale, and sat for some minutes silent. At length in a low, husky voice, he said, 'You will not be likely to speak of this, and it is well, for it must not be known. I shall satisfy myself if what you have told me is true. If I find that it is, I shall know what to do. You may go.'

"I took the book to my mistress, and was sent by her to find Zilpha. She was in the garden with Ida, and when I called her, she came bounding towards me with such a bright, happy face, that I could scarcely restrain my tears. Zilpha was a beautiful reader. She often read aloud to her mistress, by the hour together. I liked to take my sewing and sit with them at such times, but that day I was glad to shut myself up alone in my room.

"The next day the master sent for me to the library. 'It is true, Phillis,' he said to me, 'Jerry is without doubt poor Elsie's child.' If an arrow had pierced my heart at that moment, I could not have felt worse, for though I had thought I was sure it was so, all the while a hope was lingering in my heart that I was mistaken. I did not speak, and the master seeing how I trembled, kindly told me to sit down, and went on; 'I did not see Jerry myself, he said, Mr. Minturn made all necessary inquiries for me. Jerry remembers his mother, and describes her in a way that admits of no mistake. He remembers, too, that a gentleman used sometimes to visit his mother, who took a great deal of notice of him, and would let him sit upon his lap and play with his watch seals. His mother used to be very happy when this gentleman came, and when he went away she would almost smother the little boy with kisses, and talk to him of his papa. I offered to buy Jerry, but Mr. Minturn would not part with him. If he would have consented, I might easily have disposed of the whole matter.'

"A horrible fear took possession of me at these words. Would he *dare* to sell my darling Zilpha? The thought almost maddened me. Scarce knowing what I did, I threw myself on my knees before him, and begged him not to think a second time of selling his own flesh and blood. He angrily bade me rise, and not meddle with that in which I had no concern. That he had a right, which he should exercise, to do what he would with his own. He had thought it proper, he said, to tell me what I had just heard, but charged me never again to name the subject to any living being, and not to let any one suspect from my appearance that anything unusual had occurred. With this he dismissed me.

"What I suffered during that dreadful week, is known only to God. I could neither eat nor sleep. It seemed to me I should lose my reason.

"Jerry came once to Oak Grove, but I would not see him. Zilpha I avoided as much as possible. I could not bear to look upon her innocent happiness, knowing as I did that it would soon be changed into unspeakable misery.

"The first three days the master was away from home. On Thursday he returned. When I chanced to meet him, he looked uneasy; and if he came to his wife's room and found me with her, he would make some excuse for sending me away.

"Saturday was a beautiful bright October day, and Ida proposed to Zilpha that they should take their books and spend the forenoon in the woods. They went off in high spirits. I thought I had never seen my Zilpha look so lovely. Love and happiness had added a softer grace to her whole being. I followed them to the door, and she kissed me twice before leaving me; then looking back, when she had gone a little way, and seeing me still standing there, she threw a kiss to me with her little hand, and looked so bright and joyous, that my aching heart felt a new pang of sorrow. What was it whispered to me then that I should never see her again?

"I went back to my work, and presently the master came and asked for Ida. He wished her to ride with him. I told him where she was, and he went in search of her. Zilpha did not come back with them. 'We told her to stay if she wished,' Ida said. But my heart misgave me. I should at once have gone in search of her, but Mrs. Lee wanted me, and I could not go.

"I cannot bear, even now, to recall the events of that day. My worst fears were realized. During my master's absence, he had sold my darling to a Southern trader, who only waited a favorable opportunity to take her away without the knowledge of the family. He had been that morning with Mr. Lee, and was in the house when Mr. Lee returned with Ida from the woods.

"I don't know how the master ever satisfied his wife and Ida about Zilpha's disappearance. There was a report that she had run away. But I don't think they believed it. Certainly *I* never did.

"I almost forgot my own sorrow when I saw how poor Jerry felt when he knew what had happened. Of course he did not know what I did. He *never* knew why Zilpha was sent away, but he knew she was sold, and that there was little reason to hope he should ever see her again. He went about his work as usual, but there was a look in his eye which made one tremble.

"Before many days he was missing, and though his master searched the country, and took every possible means to find him, he could discover no trace of the fugitive. I felt satisfied he had followed the North Star, but I said nothing, and was glad the poor fellow had gone from what would constantly remind him of Zilpha.

"During the following winter, Mrs. Lee had a dangerous illness. I watched over her night and day, and when she recovered, my master was so grateful for what I had done, that he gave me my freedom, and money enough to bring me to the North.

"Of Zilpha's fate I have been able to learn nothing. I can only leave her with God, who though his vengeance is long delayed, hears and treasures up every sigh and tear of his poor slave-children.

"I saw, a few days since, a man who knows Jerry. He is living not many miles from me, and I shall try to see him before I die. But I shall never tell him the whole extent of the wrongs he suffered in slavery."

Annie Parker.

STORY TELLING.

BY ANNIE PARKER.

The winter wind blew cold, and the snow was falling fast,
But within the cheerful parlor none listened to the blast;
The fire was blazing brightly, and soft lamps their radiance shed
On rare and costly pictures, and many a fair young head.

The father in the easy chair, to his youngest nestling dove,
Whispered a wondrous fairy tale, such as all children love;
Brothers and sisters gathered round, and the eye might clearly trace
A happiness too deep for words, on the mother's lovely face.

And when the fairy tale was done, the blue-eyed Ella said,
"Mama, please tell a story, too, before we go to bed,
And let it be a funny one, such as I like to hear,
'Red Riding Hood,' or 'The Three Bears,' or 'Chicken Little-dear.'"

A smile beamed on the mother's face, as the little prattler spoke,
And kissing her soft, rosy cheek, she thus the silence broke,
"I will tell you, my own darlings, a story that is true,
Of a little Southern maiden, with a skin of sable hue.

"Xariffe, her mother called her, a child of beauty rare,
With soft gazelle-like eyes, and curls of dark and shining hair,
A fairy form of perfect grace, and such artless winning ways
That none who saw her, e'er could fail her loveliness to praise.

"She sported mid the orange-groves in gleeful, careless play,
And her mother, as she gazed on her, in agony would pray,
'My Father, God! be merciful! my cherished darling save
From the curse whose sum of bitterness is to be a female slave.'"

"God heard her prayer, but often He in wisdom doth withhold
The boon we crave, that we may be pure and refined like gold;
And the mother saw Xariffe grow in loveliness and grace,
Till the roses of five summers blushed in beauty on her face.

"At length, one day, one sunny day, when earth and heaven were bright,
The mother to her daily toil went forth at morning light;
At evening, when her task was done,—how can the tale be told?
She came back to her empty hut, to find her darling sold.

"Come nearer, my own precious ones, your soft white arms entwine

Around my neck, and kiss me close, sweet Ella, daughter mine;
Five years in beauty *thou* hast bloomed, of my happy life a part,
Oh, God! I guess the anguish of that lone slave-mother's heart.

"Now, darlings, go and kiss papa, and whisper your good-night,
Then hasten to your little beds, and sleep till morning light;
But oh! before you close your eyes, God's care and blessing crave,
On the saddest of His children, that poor heartbroken slave."

Annie Parker.

THE MAN-OWNER.

A FRIEND of mine, on the — — day of — —, 18—, (the dates it is unnecessary to specify,) became the owner of a man. He had never owned one before; and he has had so much trouble with him, that I doubt if he will ever allow himself to become owner of one again. My friend is not a Southerner; yet the circumstances by which so singular a dispensation fell to him, it is unnecessary for me to recount. I will briefly describe the master and the man, and show how they succeeded in their relationship.

The master was wholly respectable in his life and character; endowed with good sense; well enough off in the world, able to hire service, if he needed, and to pay for it: his temper not bad, though sometimes irritable;—he could be provoked as others can. He had strong passions, and sometimes in the course of his life they had got the better of him, and had led him to conduct which, in the coolness of his mind, he bitterly repented. Circumstances might have made a bad man of him. The instructions which he received in his childhood, the example of his parents, the respectable neighborhood in which he resided, the church which he attended, all had a favorable influence upon him. So he became a man of principle. He had not, indeed, the highest principles; he was no hero; he was not disposed to make himself a martyr. His religion was no other than the common religion of the church to which he was attached, and it demanded no peculiar sacrifice of him. He was a member of one of the leading political parties, and did his full duty in maintaining its cause. He called himself a patriot, however, not a partizan; and talked ever of his country, as the highest exemplification of the great principles of liberty, and considered the success of our institutions as the hope of humanity. Yet he loved his country,—not his race. He was not without charity to the poor; and was not unwilling to see them, individually, rising above destitution. Yet he did not like to associate with men lower in the social scale than himself; but had an ambition that impelled him to court the society of those whose station and influence were superior to his own. Nor did he care for, or believe in, any suggestions or plans, the object of which was the elevation of the poor as a class, and the levelling upwards of the human race. He thought that as a divine authority has declared to us, "ye have the poor with you always," it was ordained that we should always have them,—that they were an exceedingly useful class, as a foundation in society, that the prosperous men of the world could not do without them, and that it was not best to give them too much hope of rising.

Perhaps you will say I have given you no very definite description of him. You will think, perhaps, were I called to write of him again, I might, at once, better make use of the words of the poet,

> The annals of the human race,
> Their ruins, since the world began,
> Of him afford no other trace
> Than this,—THERE LIVED A MAN!

I fear, however, that I shall be unable to be more particular in my description of the servant; It is said, "like master, like man," and, indeed, leaving out the expressions above, which show the relationship of the master to the community and the church, the description of temper and of general, moral, and religious principle, would answer to be repeated now. Suffice it to say, the man was not bad; that is, not thoroughly bad. He cherished no secret desire for liberty. His master had no real fear of his attempting to escape. He loved his master; and some thought, who did not wholly know him, that never slave loved a master with more fondness and devotion. Yet I know that he was often disobedient. Passages,—not of arms,—but of ill-temper, of reproach, and of insolence, not unfrequently occurred between them. High words were used, hard looks and moody oftener still, perhaps, yet the master never struck his servant, nor did the servant ever offer violence towards his master. But at times, they would have been very glad to part company, if the one could have easily escaped, or the other could have made out to do without him. Much of the disobedience which gave serious offence to the master, was the result of inadvertence. Lessons, the most frequently enjoined, were forgotten; they were not always listened to with an obedient mind. Years long the master required this or that service from day to day, and yet the command was not once a year, I may say, attended to. Always the master was saying,—"to-morrow I shall turn over a new leaf with him;" but he had not energy enough to carry his purpose into effect. He intended to give his servant at least some moral education, to teach him self-control, to prevent his bursts of passion, not by the infliction of punishment, but by a true moral discipline; yet the work was always delayed, and never accomplished. You will say, the master had himself some idle fancies that he ought not to have indulged, and that a severer course would have been more successful. But he was one of those who doubt the advantages and shrink from the application of severity, and he would have been no more prompt and resolute and persevering with his servant than with himself.

At the commencement, I seemed to promise a story. But all my narrative is closed with a word more. The master was at the age of twenty-one, when he came into possession of his man. The connection will never be dissolved, except, at least, by death. Indeed, reader, if you have not already seen it, master and man were but one and the same person.

And this is the moral of my little fiction. Who will believe that any man ought to have the ownership of another, when it is so rare to find one of us wholly competent to govern and to own himself? Nay, the better a man is, and the more qualified to direct and to govern others with absolute sway, the less is he willing to take the responsibility of the disposal of them,—but seeing his own unfitness for the office of lord, even of himself, he prays, not that he may be a master of others, but himself a servant of God.

Rev. E. Buckingham

CAMBRIDGE, MASS., OCT., 1852.

DAMASCUS IN 1851.

No city has been more variously described than Damascus, because none has more contrasted features. A spruce Yankee, hearing "Silk Buckingham's" description of his "Paradise," and seeing merely narrow, half-paved, mat-covered streets, and dirty, mud-walled buildings, would prefer his native "Slabtown" to the "most refreshing scene in all our travels." And yet Damascus is one of the wonders of the world, unrivalled in what is peculiarly its own, admitting no comparison with any existing city, revelling in a beauty and a splendor belonging to Islamism more than Christianity, characterizing the age of the Caliphs rather than of the Crystal Palace.

In antiquity it has no rival. Nineveh, Babylon, Palmyra, its contemporaries, have wholly perished; while this oldest inhabited place has lost none of its population, yielded none of its local preëminence, abandoned but one of the arts for which it was so renowned, and taken not a tinge of European thought, worship, life. It numbers not far from one hundred and fifty thousand souls, of whom twenty thousand may be Greek and Armenian Christians. It lies in an exquisite garden at the foot of Anti-Lebanon, in a plain of inexhaustible fertility, watered by innumerable brooklets from those ancient streams "Abana and Pharphar," and shut in by vast groves of walnut and poplar, a "verdurous wall of Paradise," which are all that the traveller sees for hours as he draws near the city of "Abraham's steward."

Originally the seat of a renowned kingdom, and once the capital of the Saracen empire, it is now the centre of an Ottoman Pashalik, but virtually the metropolis of Syria, as it was in the earliest time. Miss Martineau and some others carelessly give it a length of seven miles; but the real extent of the city-walls in any one direction is not more than two. The gardens and groves around, however, take the same name, and are over twenty miles in circuit, of a studied, picturesque wildness, shaded lanes, running side by side with merry brooks, the whole overshadowed by the deepest forest, and forming delicious relief from the sunburnt plains of Syria. Besides the walnut, so much prized for its fruit all through the East, and the poplar, the main dependence for building, the famous damson, or Damascene plum, abounds the citron, orange, and pomegranate spread their fruit around the vine is everywhere seen, and only three miles off stands the forest of damask rose-trees whence the most delicious attar is made. But a genuine American will prefer the walnut-tree to all others, because of its freedom of growth, massiveness of trunk, depth of shade, and impressive reminiscence of home. These trees, together with the mulberry, do very much for the commerce of the city. But, indeed, Damascus is the chief depot of manufactures for Syria. Silk goods cannot be bought to such advantage elsewhere, nor of such antique patterns, nor of genuine "damask" colors. The business has suffered somewhat of late, because Turkish husbands

DAMASCUS IN 1851.

discovering that English prints are so much cheaper, and their wives fancying the flowing calicoes to be so much prettier than the patterns which their grandmothers wore, foreign goods are supplanting the domestic; and a macadamized road is contemplated from the city to its seaport Beiroot, whose effect would be to make British and French manufactures still more common, but, at the same time, to give free circulation to the handicraft of Damascus. As at Constantinople, Cairo, and elsewhere, each trade occupies its own quarter, the jewellers, pipe-makers, silk-dealers, grocers, saddlers, having each their exclusive neighborhood; none of the Bazars are such noble edifices as cluster around the mosque of St. Sophia; and in the rainy season (that is, during their winter) the pavement is so wretched and slippery, and such a mass of mud and water oozes down from the rotten awnings, that one does no justice to the unequalled richness of some of the fabrics and the grandeur of some of the khans. One traveller informs the public that there is a grand "Bazar for wholesale business" of variegated black and white marble, "surmounted by an ample dome," with a lively fountain in the centre. There are *thirty-one* such buildings, which *we* should call Exchanges, bearing each the name of the Sultan who erected them. Those that I visited were contiguous to the only street which wears a name in the East, and that name, familiar to us in the book of Acts, "Strait," Dritto, as your guide mumbles the word, a long avenue containing the only hotel in the city.

An oriental peculiarity which makes the large towns exceedingly interesting is, that every occupation is carried on out of doors, and right under your eyes as you stroll along. Here the silk web is stretched upon the outside wall of some extended building; here the butcher is dressing the meat, perhaps for your dinner, right upon the sidewalk; and here a sort of extempore sausage is cooking, so that one might almost eat it as he walks, a capital idea for hasty eaters, and a very nice article in its way. There is no other part of the world where so much cooking is to be seen all the while, and such loads of sweetmeats gladden the eyes of childhood, and such luscious compounds, scented with attar, spread temptation before every sense. The business of "El-Shans" might almost be headed by the five hundred public bakers, though the silk is still the principal manufacture, and there are reported to be seven hundred and forty-eight dealers in damask, thirty-four silk-winders, one hundred silk dyers, and one hundred and forty-three weavers of the same article.

The famous Damascus blades are nothing but an "antiquity" now,—they are uniformly called so by the people, were offered to our purchase in very small quantities by persons who knew nothing of their manufacture, at exorbitant prices, and in very uncouth forms. They appeared to be curiosities to them, as they certainly were to us, and are said to be sometimes manufactured in England. A mace, offered for sale among these scimetars of wavy steel, smacked of the Crusaders' time, and was richly inlaid with gold; the fire-arms, or blunderbusses, were grotesque and unwieldy, richly mounted, and gorgeously ornamented.

An attempt is making in certain quarters to persuade the civilized world that Turkey has still some military power. Of this almost imperial city the citadel is but a mass of ruins. Count Guyon, a confederate general with Kossuth, and now a

Turkish Pasha and drill-officer, assured us it would be repaired and strengthened; but the city-walls offer no defence against a modern army; and the Turkish soldier, notwithstanding his courage and endurance, cannot be bastinadoed into military science; neither have educated Christian officers, like Guyon, any real influence. I frequently saw the sentinels asleep while upon duty, and recent experience has proved them incapable of standing before a far smaller amount of really trained troops. Some of the barracks at Damascus are rather the finest which the Sultan possesses, and among the best in the world,—some, too, of the military exercises are pursued with a creditable zeal,—but, on the whole, a more slatternly corps of men was never seen, nor one less confident in themselves.

The christian curiosities of this oldest of inhabited cities, begin with the mosque of peculiar sanctity, once the site of St. John's Cathedral, whose chamber of relics, containing a pretended head of the Baptist, is inaccessible even to Mussulmen, the priesthood excepted. Six huge Corinthian columns, once a part of its proud portico, are built into houses and stores, so that you get but faint glimpses of their beauty and size until you mount the flat mud-roof of the modern buildings and look down into the vast area of the temple, six hundred and fifty-feet by one hundred and fifty; and there find towering above you these massive, blackened remains of Christian architecture,—significant emblems of the triumph of the Crescent over the Cross,—and yet by their imperishableness a promise of renewed glory in some brighter future. That Islamism is hastening to decay is shown impressively enough in the grand dervish mosque and khan, once quite celebrated as the Syrian enthronement of this advanced guard of Mohammed; now nothing could seem more deserted, one minaret is threatening to fall, the spacious garden is all weed-grown, and few are left to mourn over the reverse: these banner-men of the prophet, no longer warriors, students, and apostles, do but beg their bread and drone their prayers, and exchange the reputation of fanatics for that of hypocrites; they are in fact monks of the mosque, like their brothers in celibacy, changing sadly enough from enthusiasm to formality, from the fervor of first love to the grave-like chillness of an exhausted ritual.

St. Paul is of course the great name at Damascus; and your dragoman is very certain always as to the place where he was lowered down the city-wall; then he takes you to the tomb of the soldier who befriended him, close at hand, and to the little underground chapel where the Apostle's sight was restored. But having passed in turn under the sceptre of Assyrian, Babylonian, Persian, Jew, Roman, Arabian, Turk, every stone of these buildings could tell a most interesting tale, and every timber of the wall could answer with an experience corresponding to the out-door revolution.

But the grand attractions in this "Flower of the Levant and Florence of Turkey" are the coffee-houses, and the palaces of the rich. The writer of Eothen, I think it is, says, "there is one coffee-house at Damascus capable of containing a hundred persons:" a Damascus friend, a resident clergyman, carried me into one where he had himself seen, three thousand people on a gala-day, and several where hundreds of visitors would not make a crowd. This great necessity of Turkish life, this deliverance from the loneliness of an oriental home, this luxurious substitute for the daily newspaper, is carried to perfection here. First of all, comes the lofty dome-covered hall, surrounded by couches like beds, enlivened on all festivals by the Arabian Improvisator with his song and his tale; back of this are a number of rude arbors interlaced with noble shade-trees, and watered profusely by nimble brooks, the whole lighted every night by little pale lamps. These are the gossiping places for the Damascene gentlemen; where the fragrant tchébouque, the cool narghilch, or water-pipe, the delicious coffee, the indolent game at dominos, (I never saw chess played at the east,) is relieved by such domestic anecdotes as, according to my American friend, brand the domestic life of the city with beastly sensuality.

One would fain hope that these are the prejudices of an earnest missionary,— but until the residence of years had given familiarity with the language, any opinions of a visitor would be erroneous as well as presuming. Nothing, however, can bring back so powerfully the Arabian tales of enchantment as the interior of the wealthier Damascus houses. The outside is always mean and forbidding. You have sometimes to stoop under the rude, low gate; and the first court, surrounded only by servants' rooms, has nothing of interest. But the second and third quadrangles become more and more spacious, and are always of variegated marble, containing a perpetually playing fountain, overhung by the orange, the citron, and the vine, whose fragrance floats dreamily on the moist air, lulling the senses to repose. The grand saloon I found to be always arranged pretty much the same. A lower part of the pavement near the door, is the place of deposit for slippers, shoes, and the pattens which Damascus women use so much in the winter, articles all of them never intended for ornament, and never fitted to the foot, but worn as loose as possible, and never within the sitting-room, but simply as a protection from out-door wet and soil. The lower portion of the room and its rug-strewn floor are of variegated marbles, then comes curiously carved woods, then painted stucco, decorated with mirrors rising to the distant gay-colored roof. The immense loftiness, the moist coolness, the gorgeous hues, the emblazoned texts from the Koran, the sweet murmur of the various fountains, the fragrance of the orange groves, succeed to the out-door dreariness like a dream of Haroun Al Raschid to the wearied pilgrim on desert sands. The divan, or wide sofa, on three sides of this hall, is far more agreeable in this enervating climate than any European furniture; only, in winter, as the ground underneath is permeated by leaky clay tubes bearing the waters of the Barrady, and there is no other heating apparatus save a brazer of charcoal, one is sometimes very chilly, and is tempted to exchange this tomblike dampness for a cozy corner near some friendly stove or familiar fire-place.

But the general impression which unintelligent strangers carries from Damascus is, that the people have what they want, and have gone wisely to work to realize their idea of earthly blessedness,—an indolent, sensual, dreamy one to you, but in their eyes no faint type of the Mussulman's heaven.

Rev. F W Holland

CAMBRIDGE, MASS.

RELIGIOUS, MORAL, AND POLITICAL DUTIES.

What is morally wrong, cannot be made practically right. The laws of morality are taught in the Bible. They are unchangeable truths. No sophistry, no expediency, no compromise can set them aside.

If politics is the science of government, and if civil government is a divine institution, intended to protect the rights of all; if "an injury done to the meanest subject, is an injury done to the whole body;" and if "rulers must be just, ruling in the fear of God," all legislation should be based on moral duty. Any enactments that have not this basis, are, in the Divine sight, null and void. If man is endowed by nature with inalienable rights, no legislation can rightfully wrest them from him. Any attempt to do it, is an infraction of the moral law. Our religious, moral, and political duties are identical and inseparable. It is the duty of all christian legislators so to act *now*, as they know all must act, when truth and righteousness shall have a universal prevalence on the earth.

Lindley Murray Moore.

WHY SLAVERY IS IN THE CONSTITUTION.

THAT the constitution of a country should guide its action is a *truism* which none, perhaps, will be inclined to controvert. Indeed, so thoroughly is this sentiment inwrought into us, that we generally expect *practice* will conform to the constitution. But does not this subject States or nations to misapprehension by others? South Carolina, for instance, abolishes the writ of *habeas corpus* with regard to the colored people, and imprisons them, although citizens of the other States, when they enter her borders in any way. Now these are direct violations of the constitution of the United States, so direct, that they cannot be explained away. Nor do we think that South Carolina even attempts it. She openly says, that it is owing to the existence of slavery among them, that the *free* colored man, coming into contact with the slaves, will taint them with notions of liberty which will make them discontented,—that therefore her own preservation, the first law of nature, requires her to do everything she can to keep the disturbing force out of her limits, even if she have to violate the constitution of the United States. This she asserts, too, when, at the formation of the constitution, she was one of the large slave-holding States,—when she had before her the example of every nation that had practised slavery, and when now her senators and representatives in Congress are sworn to support the constitution of the Union. Thus we see that it would be doing injustice to the constitution, were we to judge of it by the practice of South Carolina.

But the inquirer will not be satisfied with the South Carolina reason. He wants something more and better. He says, too, that these give good occasion to those exercising the powers of the government to confirm all law-abiding citizens in the belief that they are well protected by the constitution, and to let the world see how much the United States prize it. But supposing he were told that those who control the government feel, in this matter, with South Carolina,—that those who had the control of the government had no power to coerce South Carolina to perform her duty,—indeed, in a partizan view, that the person injured were *no* party,—that, as a general thing, they could not even vote,—were unimportant, nay, insignificant. If those reasons will not satisfy him, he must be content with them, for it is not likely that he will get any other. We further see that injustice would be done by considering the *practice* of a people as fairly representing their constitution.

A constitution,—the organic-law,—in truth, all other law is, in some degree, a restraint on men. It makes an umpire of right,—of reason,—which, if not the same in degree in all of us, is the same in nature. Yet it must be, to some extent, a restraint on the desires or selfish passions of men. In fact, it is only carrying out the rule of doing to others what they should do to us, and tends not only to preserve, but advance society. If no constitution or law agreeing with it existed, men would be left to the sway of their own passions—nearly always selfish—and they being many and very different in different persons, sometimes, indeed, altogether opposite, and of various intensity,—would, by their indulgence, tend to confusion, to the deterioration of society, and to its ultimate dissolution.

Now the people of the United States, without the least hesitation declare,—and they fully believe it—that we are the freest nation on earth. Other nations, doubtless, with equal sincerity say of themselves the same thing. In England where, as in other countries of the old world, there is a crowded population, raising to a high price everything eatable, the *operatives*, as they are called, find it difficult to sustain life. They work all the time they can, and, even after doing this, they sometimes perish for want of such food as a human being ought to eat. No one will say that affairs are well ordered here. Having no such state of things ourselves—for except in some of our large cities, no one starves to death—we think that to suffer one to die in this way is cruel and heartless. And we greatly upbraid them for it.

But here we have slavery,—a vicious usage which European nations, excepting one, have long since laid aside. This they have done not only because it was productive of innumerable visible evils, but because it greatly and injuriously affected the character of all concerned in it, and in this way the character of the whole community,—making one part of it proud and imperious,—another suppliant and servile. They upbraid us with it, as being more inconsistent with the high principles we profess, than any act tolerated among them is or can be with the principles they profess. Then whilst we wonder that with so much wealth as England unquestionably has, she should suffer her operatives to die for something to eat, she wonders that slavery—the worst thing known among men—should be permitted to raise its head, not only as high as the many good and exalted things we possess, but above them, making them, when necessary, give way to it and even contribute to its support. Indeed, it appears to them like Satan appearing in company with the sons of God, to accuse and try one of his children.

But all this is of no avail. It produces no satisfying results,—in fact nothing but mutual ill-will and irritation. It is no difficult thing to select from the *practices* of many people such as are not what they ought to be,—still the theory, the foundation of the government may be opposed to them, but may be unable to put them down. They may exist in spite of it, and in entire opposition to its *main* object. Indeed, it appears to be much like reasoning in a circle. We come to no end,—no conclusion. To come to any satisfactory end,—any useful conclusion,—we must take something permanent,—something believed by both to be unchangeably right and moral, and compare our governments with it. Whichever comes nearest to the standard agreed on by both, must of course be nearest right. But what shall this be? Now as it is utterly in vain for one to be happy unless he conform to the laws of his being, so it is in vain that governments are instituted unless they aim to secure the happiness and safety of the governed,—the people. The peculiar benefit or enrichment of those that administer the laws, has nothing to do with good government. Then it ought, by all means, to resemble the Divine government. We do not mean a *theocracy* as it has been administered, the worst, perhaps, of all governments,—but it should be remarkable for its sacred regard to justice and right.

WHY SLAVERY IS IN THE CONSTITUTION.

But it is objected, this deals with persons as individuals and not as members of the body politic, and that all Christ's exhortations were of this kind. Well, be it so,—what of it? There is not the least danger, if one will acquit himself well in his various relations as an individual,—a MAN,—but what he will make a good citizen.

Taking this as our standard, and recurring for a moment to the assertion of our superior happiness as a people—an assertion sometimes regarded as the boastful grandiloquence of our people—is it not true that our government, *our constitution of government we mean*, more nearly resembles the Divine government than any other does, and *therefore*, that those under it *are* more happy? Some, while they are inclined to admit the fact of our superior happiness, yet seem rather to attribute it to our great abundance of land than to the nature of the government. We do not wish, in any way, to deny or even to neutralize this statement about the abundance of our land, but still it is one of the *facts* of the government,—the government was made with this in view,—it constitutes a subject for its action, and it makes of it a strong auxiliary. This, though undeniably a *great* cause, is not, in our judgment, the *chief* one. It is intellect,—mind united to such feelings and desires that most advance others to be like God in intelligence and worth,—that makes the chief cause. Where this *is* not,—or is not called forth and put into activity, nothing to purpose can be done. Indeed, it is the most powerful agent for good anywhere to be found,—for it is behind all others, and sets all others to work.

We have among us here no form of religion, as they have in other countries, to which one must conform before he can have any share in the government,—no religion that is made part of the government, and which is, therefore, *national*. Religion—how we shall serve or worship a Being or beings superior to ourselves, and who are thought to influence our destiny forever—is, certainly, the highest concern of man. As no church or nation can answer for him at the judgment-seat, he ought to be left free on this matter. On this point he is free in this country, he is under no necessity to think in a particular channel. In his inquiries after truth, he has nothing to fear from the government about the changes through which his mind may pass, or the conclusions to which it maybe led; although he may draw on him the prejudice and hatred of the sects from whom he feels compelled to differ.[18] We may truly say, that in this country, however far we may go in imitating foreign forms, we have nothing higher than the preacher of the truth.

We have no monarch *born* to rule over us, whether we will or not; nor are we obliged to support this costly leech according to *his* dignity by money wrung from the labor of the country, nor a host of relatives according to *their* dignity, as connected with the monarch.

Nor have we a class *born* to be our legislators. We have no legislative castes, nor social castes, but we may truly say, that any native-born citizen of the United States may aspire to any position, be it governmental or social.

---

[18] It is vain to say that rich governments cannot, and do not, offer effective temptations to clever and eloquent men, whose religious views differ from the national form, to induce them to adopt the latter.

Nor have we fought so long—though it must be confessed we are ready pupils here—as most of the countries of the old world have; still we begin to make fighting almost a part of the government, and a part of the religion of the land. But all this does not answer the question that many have asked, and that our intelligence and exemption from bias in many things make more remarkable,—why did we suffer slavery to find a place in a constitution in which there are so many good things,—why did we make a garden of healthful fruits and enchanting flowers, and place this serpent in it?

The answer to this question may be easily given by one that well knows the condition of the country that soon followed on the treaty of 1783. Till we were governed by the present constitution we were governed by the Articles of Confederation. The United States, though nominally a nation, had no power to enforce any stipulation she might make. For instance,—if she should promise by a treaty to pay interest on the debt that we had contracted to secure our national independence, each State by its *own* power and authority were to raise its quota of the whole amount. If a State failed to raise it, the *United States* had no redress. It had no authority to coerce any State, no matter what was the cause of failure. This is given as only an instance, and did we not think it made our position very plain, others might be given in manifold abundance,—all tending to show the unfaithfulness of the States to the engagements of the United States, and the utter powerlessness of the latter to keep her word. It was owing to this that the *main* object of the Convention was the more perfect union of the States, and that in this way there might be conferred on the United States the same plenary power to carry out her engagements that a State had to carry out hers.

The Convention did not meet to do away with slavery, but chiefly to form such a union as would obviate the difficulty already mentioned, and so keenly felt by some of the most earnest friends of the country. Although slavery was pretty well understood then, and seen to be opposed to all the principles of freedom asserted, yet as it had been embraced by so many, that if they should be united against the constitution its adoption would be endangered, it was thought best not to insist on its instant abolition. Men as yet had too much selfishness in them, and although reasonable beings, they have too much of the animal in them to see that, in the long run, honesty is the best policy. Many of the opponents of slavery, even from the slave States themselves, took this opportunity of showing the baseness and turpitude of the whole system,—its advocates from the far South defending it as well as they could. These advocates gave it as their opinion, that owing to the Declaration of 1776, one which had already done wonders at the North,—owing to the influence of the principles of liberty inserted into the constitution, and to the feeling of justice pervading all classes of persons, and to the progress of refinement and true civilization, slavery would ultimately disappear.[19]

[19] Congress, the legislative department, and, of course, the judicial, its interpreter, were intended to be founded on such undoubted principles of liberty, that it would be difficult for them to use their everywhere acknowledged rights, and perform their everywhere expected duties, without first putting aside the strongest impediment to their exercise, slavery. In our judgment this has been done. There is no truth in public law more certain than that protection and allegiance are reciprocal. They must exist together or not at all. The

WHY SLAVERY IS IN THE CONSTITUTION.

At the time this opinion was expressed by the conventionists from the South, although we cultivated cotton to a small extent, it could not be regarded as a staple. Soon after making the constitution, it began to be important. It could be produced only at the South. As it grew in value, the notion of abolishing slavery began to wane, till now some of the leading men of that part of the country say it is not only a good thing, but an indispensable one to the highest perfection of the social system.

James G. Birney.

James G. Birney.

---

power of the United States is adequate for the protection of all within her limits, and from all within them she expects allegiance. If she is informed in any way to be relied on, that any person is restrained of his rights under the constitution of the United States, it is her duty to see him set at liberty, if he be confined, and see that he is redressed. It is in vain for Congress to excuse itself from acting, by saying that it is a *State* concern. Can a citizen of the *United States*, if he be a citizen, be tortured or tormented by a *State*, when there is no pretence that he has violated the law of either?

The constitution of the United States authorizes no man to hold another as a slave. The United States has no power to hold a slave. It matters not that it was *intended* to allow some to hold others as their slaves. A very vile person may *intend* to lock up in prison an innocent and just one, but through mistake he leaves the door unlocked; does this, in the eyes of any reasonable men, prevent his making his escape through the door? We are certain not. The only proper inquiry here is, which is supreme, the government of the Union, or the government of a particular State of it. It is not necessary to answer this. If the first deal with no one as a slave, the subordinate cannot by law. Persons may be held as slaves by fraud, by cunning, by taking advantage of the ignorance in which we hold them, by force, or a successful combination of force, but not by LAW.

THE TWO ALTARS;
OR,
TWO PICTURES IN ONE.

BY MRS. HARRIET BEECHER STOWE.

I.—THE ALTAR OF LIBERTY, OR 1776.

THE well-sweep of the old house on the hill was relieved, dark and clear, against the reddening sky, as the early winter sun was going down in the west. It was a brisk, clear, metallic evening; the long drifts of snow blushed crimson red on their tops, and lay in shades of purple and lilac in the hollows; and the old wintry wind brushed shrewdly along the plain, tingling people's noses, blowing open their cloaks, puffing in the back of their necks, and showing other unmistakable indications that he was getting up steam for a real roystering night.

"Hurra! how it blows!" said little Dick Ward, from the top of the mossy wood-pile.

Now Dick had been sent to said wood-pile, in company with his little sister Grace, to pick up chips, which, every-body knows, was in the olden time considered a wholesome and gracious employment, and the peculiar duty of the rising generation. But said Dick, being a boy, had mounted the wood-pile, and erected there a flag-staff, on which he was busily tying a little red pocket-handkerchief, occasionally exhorting Gracie "to be sure and pick up fast." "O, yes, I will," said Grace; "but you see the chips have got ice on 'em, and make my hands so cold!"

"O! don't stop to suck your thumbs!—who cares for ice? Pick away, I say, while I set up the flag of Liberty."

So Grace picked away as fast as she could, nothing doubting but that her cold thumbs were in some mysterious sense an offering on the shrine of Liberty; while soon the red handkerchief, duly secured, fluttered and snapped in the brisk evening wind.

"Now you must hurra, Gracie, and throw up your bonnet," said Dicky, as he descended from the pile.

"But won't it lodge down in some place in the wood-pile?" suggested Gracie, thoughtfully.

"O, never fear; give it to me, and just holler now, Gracie, 'Hurra for Liberty;' and we'll throw up your bonnet and my cap; and we'll play, you know, that we

THE TWO ALTARS; 75

were a whole army, and I'm General Washington."

So Gracie gave up her little red hood, and Dick swung his cap, and up they both went into the air; and the children shouted, and the flag snapped and fluttered, and altogether they had a merry time of it. But then the wind—good-for-nothing, roguish fellow!—made an ungenerous plunge at poor Gracie's little hood, and snipped it up in a twinkling, and whisked it off, off, off,—fluttering and bobbing up and down, quite across a wide, waste, snowy field, and finally lodged it on the top of a tall strutting rail, that was leaning very independently, quite another way from all the other rails of the fence.

"Now see, do see!" said Gracie; "there goes my bonnet! What will Aunt Hitty say?" and Gracie began to cry.

"Don't you cry, Gracie; you offered it up to Liberty, you know,—it's glorious to give up everything for Liberty."

"O! but Aunt Hitty won't think so."

"Well, don't cry, Gracie, you foolish girl! Do you think I can't get it? Now, only play that that great rail was a fort, and your bonnet was a prisoner in it, and see how quick I'll take the fort, and get it!" and Dick shouldered a stick, and started off.

"What upon 'arth keeps those children so long? I should think they were making chips!" said Aunt Mehetabel; "the fire's just a-going out under the tea-kettle."

By this time Gracie had lugged her heavy basket to the door, and was stamping the snow off her little feet, which were so numb that she needed to stamp, to be quite sure they were yet there. Aunt Mehetabel's shrewd face was the first that greeted her, as the door opened.

"Gracie—what upon 'arth!—wipe your nose, child; your hands are frozen. Where alive is Dick, and what's kept you out all this time,—and where's your bonnet?"

Poor Gracie, stunned by this cataract of questions, neither wiped her nose nor gave any answer; but sidled up into the warm corner, where grandmamma was knitting, and began quietly rubbing and blowing her fingers, while the tears silently rolled down her cheeks, as the fire made their former ache intolerable.

"Poor little dear!" said grandmamma, taking her hands in hers; "Hitty shan't scold you. Grandma knows you've been a good girl,—the wind blew poor Gracie's bonnet away;" and grandmamma wiped both eyes and nose, and gave her, moreover, a stalk of dried fennel out of her pocket, whereat Gracie took heart once more.

"Mother always makes fools of Roxy's children," said Mehetabel, puffing zealously under the tea-kettle. "There's a little maple sugar in that saucer up there, mother, if you will keep giving it to her," she said, still vigorously puffing. "And now, Gracie," she said, when, after a while, the fire seemed in tolerable order, "will you answer my question?—Where is Dick?"

"Gone over in the lot, to get my bonnet."

"How came your bonnet off?" said Aunt Mehetabel. "I tied it on firm enough."

"Dick wanted me to take it off for him, to throw up for Liberty," said Grace.

"Throw up for fiddlestick! just one of Dick's cut-ups, and you was silly enough to mind him!"

"Why, he put up a flag-staff on the wood-pile, and a flag to Liberty, you know, that papa's fighting for," said Grace, more confidently, as she saw her quiet, blue-eyed mother, who had silently walked into the room during the conversation.

Grace's mother smiled, and said, encouragingly, "And what then?"

"Why, he wanted me to throw up my bonnet and he his cap, and shout for Liberty; and then the wind took it and carried it off, and he said I ought not to be sorry if I did lose it,—it was an offering to Liberty."

"And so I did," said Dick, who was standing as straight as a poplar behind the group; "and I heard it in one of father's letters to mother, that we ought to offer up everything on the altar of Liberty! And so I made an altar of the wood-pile."

"Good boy!" said his mother, "always remember everything your father writes. He has offered up everything on the altar of Liberty, true enough; and I hope you, son, will live to do the same."

"Only, if I have the hoods and caps to make," said Aunt Hitty, "I hope he won't offer them up every week—that's all!"

"O! well, Aunt Hitty, I've got the hood,—let me alone for that. It blew clear over into the Daddy Ward pasture-lot, and there stuck on the top of the great rail; and I played that the rail was a fort, and besieged it, and took it."

"O! yes, you're always up to taking forts, and anything else that nobody wants done. I'll warrant, now, you left Gracie to pick up every blessed one of them chips!"

"Picking up chips is girl's work," said Dick; "and taking forts and defending the country is men's work."

"And pray, Mister Pomp, how long have you been a man?" said Aunt Hitty.

"If I a'nt a man, I soon shall be; my head is 'most up to my mother's shoulder, and I can fire off a gun too. I tried, the other day, when I was up to the store. Mother, I wish you'd let me clean and load the old gun; so that, if the British should come!"

"Well, if you are so big and grand, just lift me out that table, sir," said Aunt Hitty, "for its past supper-time."

Dick sprung, and had the table out in a trice, with an abundant clatter, and put up the leaves with quite an air. His mother, with the silent and gliding motion characteristic of her, quietly took out the table-cloth and spread it, and began to set the cups and saucers in order, and to put on the plates and knives, while Aunt Hitty bustled about the tea.

"I'll be glad when the war's over, for one reason," said she. "I'm pretty much tired of drinking sage-tea, for one, I know."

"Well, Aunt Hitty, how you scolded that pedler, last week, that brought along that real tea."

"To be sure I did. S'pose I'd be taking any of his old tea, bought of the British?—fling every tea-cup in his face, first!"

"Well, mother," said Dick, "I never exactly understood what it was about the tea, and why the Boston folks threw it all overboard."

"Because there was an unlawful tax laid upon it, that the government had no right to lay. It wasn't much in itself; but it was a part of a whole system of oppressive meanness, designed to take away our rights, and make us slaves of a foreign power!"

"Slaves!" said Dicky, straightening himself proudly. "Father a slave!"

"But they would not be slaves! They saw clearly where it would all end, and they would not begin to submit to it in ever so little," said the mother.

"I wouldn't, if I was they," said Dicky.

"Besides," said his mother, drawing him towards her, "it wasn't for themselves alone they did it. This is a great country, and it will be greater and greater: and it's very important that it should have free and equal laws, because it will by and by be so great. This country, if it is a free one, will be a light of the world,—a city set on a hill, that cannot be hid; and all the oppressed and distressed from other countries shall come here to enjoy equal rights and freedom. This, dear boy, is why your father and uncles have gone to fight, and why they do stay and fight, though God knows what they suffer, and—" and the large blue eyes of the mother were full of tears; yet a strong, bright beam of pride and exultation shone through those tears.

"Well, well, Roxy, you can always talk, every-body knows," said Aunt Hitty, who had been not the least attentive listener of this little patriotic harangue; "but, you see, the tea is getting cold, and yonder I see the sleigh is at the door, and John's come,—so let's set up our chairs for supper."

The chairs were soon set up, when John, the eldest son, a lad of about fifteen, entered with a letter. There was one general exclamation, and stretching out of hands towards it. John threw it into his mother's lap;—the tea-table was forgotten, and the tea-kettle sang unnoticed by the fire, as all hands piled themselves up by mother's chair to hear the news. It was from Captain Ward, then in the American army, at Valley Forge. Mrs. Ward ran it over hastily, and then read it aloud. A few words we may extract: "There is still," it said, "much suffering. I have given away every pair of stockings you sent me, reserving to myself only one; for I will not be one whit better off than the poorest soldier that fights for his country. Poor fellows! it makes my heart ache sometimes to go round among them, and see them with their worn clothes and torn shoes, and often bleeding feet, yet cheerful and hopeful, and every one willing to do his very best. Often the spirit of discouragement comes over them, particularly at night, when, weary, cold, and hungry, they turn into their comfortless huts, on the snowy ground. Then sometimes there is a thought of home, and warm fires, and some speak of giving up; but next morning out comes Washington's general orders,—little short note, but it's wonderful the good it does! and then they all resolve to hold on, come what may. There are commissioners going all through the country to pick up supplies. If they come to you, I need not tell you what to do. I know all that will be in your hearts."

"There, children, see what your father suffers," said the mother, "and what it costs these poor soldiers to gain our liberty."

"Ephraim Scranton told me that the commissioners had come as far as the Three-mile Tavern, and that he rather 'spected they'd be along here to-night," said John, as he was helping round the baked beans to the silent company at the tea-table.

"To-night?—Do tell, now!" said Aunt Hitty. "Then it's time we were awake and stirring. Let's see what can be got."

"I'll send my new over-coat, for one," said John. "That old one an't cut up yet, is it, Aunt Hitty?"

"No," said Aunt Hitty; "I was laying out to cut it over, next Wednesday, when Desire Smith could be here to do the tailoring."

"There's the south room," said Aunt Hitty, musing; "that bed has the two old Aunt Ward blankets on it, and the great blue quilt, and two comforters. Then mother's and my room, two pair—four comforters—two quilts—the best chamber has got——"

"O! Aunt Hitty, send all that's in the best chamber. If any company comes, we can make it up off from our beds!" said John. "I can send a blanket or two off from my bed, I know;—can't but just turn over in it, so many clothes on, now."

"Aunt Hitty, take a blanket off from our bed," said Grace and Dicky, at once.

"Well, well, we'll see," said Aunt Hitty, bustling up.

Up rose grandmamma, with great earnestness, now, and going into the next room, and opening a large cedar-wood chest, returned, bearing in her arms two large snow-white blankets, which she deposited flat on the table, just as Aunt Hitty was whisking off the table-cloth.

"Mortal! mother, what are you going to do?" said Aunt Hitty.

"There," she said, "I spun those, every thread of 'em, when my name was Mary Evans. Those were my wedding blankets, made of real nice wool, and worked with roses in all the corners. I've got *them* to give!" and grandmamma stroked and smoothed the blankets, and patted them down, with great pride and tenderness. It was evident she was giving something that lay very near her heart; but she never faltered.

"La! mother, there's no need of that," said Aunt Hitty. "Use them on your own bed, and send the blankets off from that;—they are just as good for the soldiers."

"No, I shan't!" said the old lady, waxing warm; "'t an't a bit too good for 'em. I'll send the very best I've got, before they shall suffer. Send 'em the *best*!" and the old lady gestured oratorically!

THE TWO ALTARS; 79

They were interrupted by a rap at the door, and two men entered, and announced themselves as commissioned by Congress to search out supplies for the army. Now the plot thickens. Aunt Hitty flew in every direction,—through entry-passage, meal-room, milk-room, down cellar, up chamber,—her cap-border on end with patriotic zeal; and followed by John, Dick, and Gracie, who eagerly bore to the kitchen the supplies that she turned out, while Mrs. Ward busied herself in quietly sorting, bundling, and arranging in the best possible travelling order, the various contributions that were precipitately launched on the kitchen floor.

Aunt Hitty soon appeared in the kitchen with an armful of stockings, which, kneeling on the floor, she began counting and laying out.

"There," she said, laying down a large bundle on some blankets, "that leaves just two pair apiece all round."

"La!" said John, "what's the use of saving two pair for me? I can do with one pair, as well as father."

"Sure enough," said his mother; "besides, I can knit you another pair in a day."

"And I can do with one pair," said Dicky.

"Yours will be too small," young master, I guess, said one of the commissioners.

"No," said Dicky; "I've got a pretty good foot of my own, and Aunt Hitty will always knit my stockings an inch too long, 'cause she says I grow so. See here,—these will do;" and the boy shook his, triumphantly.

"And mine, too," said Gracie, nothing doubting, having been busy all the time in pulling off her little stockings.

"Here," she said to the man who was packing the things into a wide-mouthed sack; "here's mine," and her large blue eyes looked earnestly through her tears.

Aunt Hitty flew at her.—"Good land! the child's crazy! Don't think the men could wear your stockings,—take 'em away!"

Gracie looked around with an air of utter desolation, and began to cry. "I wanted to give them something," said she. "I'd rather go barefoot on the snow all day, than not send 'em anything."

"Give me the stockings, my child," said the old soldier, tenderly. "There, I'll take 'em, and show 'em to the soldiers, and tell them what the little girl said that sent them. And it will do them as much good as if they could wear them. They've got little girls at home, too." Gracie fell on her mother's bosom completely happy, and Aunt Hitty only muttered,

"Everybody does spile that child; and no wonder, neither!"

Soon the old sleigh drove off from the brown house, tightly packed and heavily loaded. And Gracie and Dicky were creeping up to their little beds.

"There's been something put on the altar of Liberty to-night, hasn't there, Dick?"

"Yes, indeed," said Dick; and, looking up to his mother, he said, "But, mother, what did you give?"

"I?" said the mother, musingly.

"Yes, you, mother; what have you given to the country?"

"All that I have, dears," said she, laying her hands gently on their heads, — "my husband and my children!"

II.—THE ALTAR OF ——, OR 1850.

The setting sun of chill December lighted up the solitary front window of a small tenement on — — street, which we now have occasion to visit. As we push gently aside the open door, we gain sight of a small room, clean as busy hands can make it, where a neat, cheerful young mulatto woman is busy at an ironing-table. A basket full of glossy-bosomed shirts, and faultless collars and wristbands, is beside her, into which she is placing the last few items with evident pride and satisfaction. A bright, black-eyed boy, just come in from school, with his satchel of books over his shoulder, stands, cap in hand, relating to his mother how he has been at the head of his class, and showing his school-tickets, which his mother, with untiring admiration, deposits in the little real china tea-pot, — which, as being their most reliable article of gentility, is made the deposit of all the money and most especial valuables of the family.

"Now, Henry," says the mother, "look out and see if father is coming along the street;" and she begins filling the little black tea-kettle, which is soon set singing on the stove.

From the inner room now daughter Mary, a well-grown girl of thirteen, brings the baby, just roused from a nap, and very impatient to renew his acquaintance with his mamma.

"Bless his bright eyes! — mother will take him," ejaculates the busy little woman, whose hands are by this time in a very floury condition, in the incipient stages of wetting up biscuit, — "in a minute;" and she quickly frees herself from the flour and paste, and, deputing Mary to roll out her biscuit, proceeds to the consolation and succor of young master.

"Now, Henry," says the mother, "you'll have time, before supper, to take that basket of clothes up to Mr. Sheldin's; — put in that nice bill, that you made out last night. I shall give you a cent for every bill you write out for me. What a comfort it is, now, for one's children to be gettin' learnin' so!"

Henry shouldered the basket, and passed out the door, just as a neatly-dressed colored man walked up, with his pail and white-wash brushes.

"O, you've come, father, have you? — Mary, are the biscuits in? — you may as well set the table, now. Well, George, what's the news?"

"Nothing, only a pretty smart day's work. I've brought home five dollars, and shall have as much as I can do, these two weeks;" and the man, having washed his hands, proceeded to count out his change on the ironing-table.

"Well, it takes you to bring in the money," said the delighted wife; "nobody but you could turn off that much in a day!"

"Well, they do say—those that's had me once—that they never want any other hand to take hold in their rooms. I s'pose its a kinder practice I've got, and kinder natural!"

"Tell ye what," said the little woman, taking down the family strong box,—to wit, the china tea-pot, aforenamed,—and pouring the contents on the table, "we're getting mighty rich, now! We can afford to get Henry his new Sunday-cap, and Mary her muslin-de-laine dress;—take care, baby, you rogue!" she hastily interposed, as young master made a dive at a dollar bill, for his share in the proceeds.

"He wants something, too, I suppose," said the father; "let him get his hand in while he's young."

The baby gazed, with round, astonished eyes, while mother, with some difficulty, rescued the bill from his grasp; but, before any one could at all anticipate his purpose, he dashed in among the small change with such zeal as to send it flying all over the table.

"Hurra!—Bob's a smasher!" said the father, delighted; "he'll make it fly, he thinks;" and, taking the baby on his knee, he laughed merrily, as Mary and her mother pursued the rolling coin all over the room.

"He knows now, as well as can be, that he's been doing mischief," said the delighted mother, as the baby kicked and crowed uproariously;—"he's such a forward child, now, to be only six months old!—O, you've no idea, father, how mischievous he grows," and therewith the little woman began to roll and tumble the little mischief-maker about, uttering divers frightful threats, which appeared to contribute, in no small degree, to the general hilarity.

"Come, come, Mary," said the mother, at last, with a sudden burst of recollection; "you mustn't be always on your knees fooling with this child!—Look in the oven at them biscuits."

"They're done exactly, mother,—just the brown!"—and, with the word, the mother dumped baby on to his father's knee, where he sat contentedly munching a very ancient crust of bread, occasionally improving the flavor thereof by rubbing it on his father's coat-sleeve.

"What have you got in that blue dish, there?" said George, when the whole little circle were seated around the table.

"Well, now, what *do* you suppose?" said the little woman, delighted;—"a quart of nice oysters,—just for a treat, you know. I wouldn't tell you till this minute," said she, raising the cover.

"Well," said George, "we both work hard for our money, and we don't owe anybody a cent; and why shouldn't we have our treats, now and then, as well as rich folks?"

And gayly passed the supper hour; the tea-kettle sung, the baby crowed, and all chatted and laughed abundantly.

"I'll tell you," said George, wiping his mouth, "wife, these times are quite another thing from what it used to be down in Georgia. I remember then old Mas'r used to hire me out by the year; and one time, I remember, I came and paid him in two hundred dollars,—every cent I'd taken. He just looked it over, counted it, and put it in his pocket-book, and said, 'You are a good boy, George,'—and he gave me *half-a-dollar!*"

"I want to know, now!" said his wife.

"Yes, he did, and that was every cent I ever got of it; and, I tell you, I was mighty bad off for clothes, them times."

"Well, well, the Lord be praised, they're over, and you are in a free country now!" said the wife, as she rose thoughtfully from the table, and brought her husband the great Bible. The little circle were ranged around the stove for evening prayers.

"Henry, my boy, you must read,—you are a better reader than your father,—thank God, that let you learn early!"

The boy, with a cheerful readiness, read, "The Lord is my shepherd," and the mother gently stilled the noisy baby, to listen to the holy words. Then all knelt, while the father, with simple earnestness, poured out his soul to God.

They had but just risen,—the words of Christian hope and trust scarce died on their lips,—when lo! the door was burst open, and two men entered; and one of them advancing, laid his hand on the father's shoulder. "This is the fellow," said he.

"You are arrested in the name of the United States!" said the other.

"Gentlemen, what is this?" said the poor man, trembling.

"Are you not the property of *Mr. B.*, of Georgia?" said the officer.

"Gentlemen, I've been a free, hard-working man, these ten years."

"Yes, but you are arrested, on suit of Mr. B., as his slave."

Shall we describe the leave-taking?—the sorrowing wife, the dismayed children, the tears, the anguish,—that simple, honest, kindly home, in a moment so desolated! Ah, ye who defend this because it is law, think, for one hour, what if this that happens to your poor brother should happen to you!*****

It was a crowded court-room, and the man stood there to be tried—for life?—no; but for the life of life—for liberty!

Lawyers hurried to and fro, buzzing, consulting, bringing authorities,—all anxious, zealous, engaged,—for what?—to save a fellow-man from bondage?—no; anxious and zealous lest he might escape,—full of zeal to deliver him over to slavery. The poor man's anxious eyes follow vainly the busy course of affairs, from which he dimly learns that he is to be sacrificed—on the altar of the Union; and that his heart-break and anguish, and the tears of his wife, and the desolation of his children, are, in the eyes of these well-informed men, only the bleat of a sacrifice, bound to the horns of the glorious American altar!****

THE TWO ALTARS;

Again it is a bright day, and business walks brisk in this market. Senator and statesman, the learned and patriotic, are out, this day, to give their countenance to an edifying and impressive, and truly American spectacle,—the sale of a man! All the preliminaries of the scene are there; dusky-browed mothers, looking with sad eyes while speculators are turning round their children,—looking at their teeth, and feeling of their arms; a poor, old, trembling woman, helpless, half-blind, whose last child is to be sold, holds on to her bright boy with trembling hands. Husbands and wives, sisters and friends, all soon to be scattered like the chaff of the threshing-floor, look sadly on each other with poor nature's last tears; and among them walk briskly glib, oily politicians, and thriving men of law, letters, and religion, exceedingly sprightly and in good spirits,—for why?—it isn't *they* that are going to be sold; it's only somebody else. And so they are very comfortable, and look on the whole thing as quite a matter-of-course affair; and, as it is to be conducted to-day, a decidedly valuable and judicious exhibition.

And now, after so many hearts and souls have been knocked and thumped this way and that way by the auctioneer's hammer, comes the *instructive* part of the whole; and the husband and father, whom we saw in his simple home, reading and praying with his children, and rejoicing, in the joy of his poor ignorant heart, that he lived in a free country, is now set up to be admonished of his mistake.

Now there is great excitement, and pressing to see, and exultation and approbation; for it is important and interesting to see a man put down that has tried to be a *free man*.

"That's he, is it?—Couldn't come it, could he?" says one.

"No, and he will never come it, that's more," says another, triumphantly.

"I don't generally take much interest in scenes of this nature," says a grave representative;—"but I came here to-day for the sake of the *principle*!"

"Gentlemen," says the auctioneer, "we've got a specimen here that some of your Northern abolitionists would give any price for; but they shan't have him!—no! we've looked out for that. The man that buys him must give bonds never to sell him to go North again!"

"Go it!" shout the crowd, "good!—good!—hurra!" "An impressive idea!" says a senator; "a noble maintaining of principle!" and the man is bid off, and the hammer falls with a last crash on his hearth, and hopes, and manhood, and he lies a bleeding wreck on the altar of Liberty!

Such was the altar in 1776;—such is the altar in 1850!

Mrs. H. B. Stowe.

OUTLINE OF A MAN.

In some of those castle-building day-dreams, in which, like all youth of an imaginative turn, I was wont, in my early days, to indulge, a favorite image of my creation was an *Africo-American for the time*,—a colored man, who had known by experience the bitterness of slavery, and now by some process free, so endowed with natural powers, and a certain degree of attainments, all the more rare and effective for being acquired under great disadvantages,—as to be a sort of Moses to his oppressed and degraded tribe. He was to be gifted with a noble person, of course, and refinement of manners, and some elegance of thought and expression; by what unprecedented miracle such a paragon was to be graduated through the educational appliances of American slavery, imagination did not trouble herself to inquire. She was painting fancy-pieces, not portraits.

Having thus irresponsibly struck out upon the canvas her central figure, she would not be slow to complete the picture with many a rose-colored vision of brilliant successes and magic triumphs won by her hero, in his great enterprise of the redemption of his people. A burning sense of their wrongs fired his eloquence with an undying, passionate earnestness, and as he alternately reproached the injustice, and appealed to the generosity of his oppressors, all opposition gave way before him; the masses, as one man, demanded the emancipation of his long-degraded, deeply injured race; and millions of regenerated men rose up, upon their broken chains and called him blessed.

Years rolled away, and these poetic fancies faded "into the light of common day." The cold, stern, pitiless reality remained. The dark incubus of slavery yet rested down upon more than three millions of the victims of democratic despotism. But the triumphant champion of the devoted race had melted away, with the morning mists of my boyish conjuring.

One morning in the summer of 1844, walking up Main-street in the city of Hartford, I was attracted by the movements of a group of some twenty-five or thirty men and women, in a small recess, or court, by the side of the old Centre Church. They appeared to be organized into an assembly, and a tall mulatto was addressing them. I drew near to listen. The speaker was recounting the oft-enacted history of a flight from slavery. With his eye upon the cold, but true north star, and his ear ever and anon bent to the ground, listening for the "blood-hound's savage bay," sure-footed and panting, the fugitive was before me! My attention had been arrested; I was profoundly interested. The audience was the American Anti-slavery Society, then just excluded from some of the public halls of the city, and fain to content themselves, after an apostolic sort, with the *next best* accommodations.

The orator was FREDERICK DOUGLASS, the most remarkable man of this country, and of this age; and—may I not dare to add—the almost complete fulfilment of my early dream!

Since that day, through assiduous application, and a varied experience, he has continued to develop in the same wonderful ratio of improvement, which even then distinguished him as a prodigy in self-education. Unusually favored in personal appearance and address, full of generous impulse and delicate sensibility, exuberant in playful wit, or biting sarcasm, or stern denunciation, ever commanding in his moral attitude, earnest and impressive in manner, with a voice eminently sonorous and flexible, and gesture full of dramatic vivacity, I have many times seen large audiences swayed at his will; at one moment convulsed with laughter, and at the next, bathed in tears; now lured with admiration of the orator, and now with indignation at the oppressor, against whom he hurled his invective. But in my boyhood's quasi-prophetic fancy of such a man and his inimitable success, I had not counted upon one antagonist, whose reality and potency, the observation of every day now forces painfully upon me. I mean the strange and unnatural *prejudice against mere color*, which is so all-prevalent in the American breast, as almost to nullify the influence of *such* a man, *so* pleading; while his dignity, his urbanity, his imperturbable serenity and good nature, his genuine purity and worth all fail, at times, to secure him from the grossest indignities, at the hands of the coarse and brutal. Nobody who knows him will be inclined to question our estimate of his character, but it still comports with the intelligence and refinement and piety of a large proportion of American society to label him "nigger," and the name itself invites to safe contumely, and irresponsible violence.

I have spoken of Frederick Douglass as an interesting man—a wonderful man. Look at him as he stands to-day before this nation; and then contemplate his history.

Begin with him when, a little slave-child, he lay down on his rude pallet, and that slave-mother, from a plantation twelve miles away, availed herself of the privilege granted grudgingly, of travelling the whole distance, after the day's work, (on peril of the lash, unless back again by sunrise to her task,) that she might lie there by his side, and sing him with her low sweet song to sleep. "I do not recollect," says he, "of ever seeing my mother by the light of day. She was with me in the night. She would lie down with me, and get me to sleep, but long before I awaked, she was gone." How touching the love of that dark-browed bondwoman for her boy! How precious must the memory of that dim but sweet remembrance be to him, who though once a vassal, bound and scourged, and still a Helot, proscribed and wronged, may not be robbed of this dear token that he, too, *had once a mother*! Her low sad lullaby yet warps his life's dark woof—for she watches over his pathway now with spirit-eyes, and still keeps singing on in his heart, and nursing his courage and his patience.

Follow him through all the tempestuous experience of his bondage. His lashings, his longings, his perseverance in possessing himself of the key of knowledge, which, after all, only unlocked to him the fatal secret that he was a slave, a thing to be bought and sold like oxen. Imagine the tumult of his soul, as standing by the broad Chesapeake, he watched the receding vessels, "while they flew on their white wings before the breeze, and apostrophized them as animated by the living spirit of freedom;"[20] or when reading in a stray copy of the old "Columbian Orator," (verily, all our school-books must be expurgated of the incendiary "perilous stuff" in which they abound,) the "Dialogue between a Master and his Slave," and Sheridan's great speech on Catholic Emancipation.[21] See to what heroic resistance his proud heart had swollen, when he turned outright upon his tormentor—pious Mr. Corey, the "nigger-breaker"—and inflicted condign retribution on his heartless ribs; "after which," says he, significantly, "I was never whipped again; *I had several fights*, but was never whipped." Attend him in his exodus from our republican Egypt. Witness his struggles with poverty; his vain attempts to find employment at his trade, as a colored man, in the *free* North. Behold him at last emerging from his obscurity at the Anti-slavery Convention in Nantucket. Somebody, who is aware of his extraordinary natural intelligence, invites him to speak. Tremblingly he consents. "As soon as he had taken his seat," said Mr. Garrison, after describing the tremendous effect of his remarks upon the audience, "filled with hope and admiration, I rose and declared that Patrick Henry, of revolutionary fame, never made a speech more eloquent in the cause of liberty, than the one we had just listened to from the hunted fugitive."

---

[20] "Our house stood within a few rods of the Chesapeake bay, whose broad bosom was ever white with sails from every quarter of the habitable globe. Those beautiful vessels, robed in purest white, so delightful to the eye of freemen, were to me so many shrouded ghosts to terrify and torment me with thoughts of my wretched condition. I have often, in the deep stillness of a summer's Sabbath, stood all alone upon the lofty banks of that noble bay, and traced, with saddened heart and tearful eye, the countless number of sails moving off to the mighty ocean. The sight of these always affected me powerfully. My thoughts would compel utterance; and then, with no audience but the Almighty, I would pour out my soul's complaint, in my rude way, with an apostrophe to the moving multitude of ships:—

"You are loosed from your moorings, and are free; I am fast in my chains, and am a slave! You move merrily before the gentle gale, and I sadly before the bloody whip! You are freedom's swift-winged angels that fly around the world; I am confined in bands of iron! O that I were free! O that I were on one of your gallant decks, and under your protecting wing! Alas! betwixt me and you the turbid waters roll. Go on, go on. O that I could also go! Could I but swim! If I could fly! O, why was I born a man, of whom to make a brute! The glad ship is gone; she hides in the dim distance. I am left in the hottest hell of unending slavery. O God, save me! God, deliver me! Let me be free! Is there any God? Why am I a slave? I will run away. * * * Only think of it; one hundred miles straight north, and I am free! Try it? Yes! God helping me, I will. It cannot be that I shall live and die a slave. * * *"—*Autobiography of Douglass*, pp. 64, 65.

[21] "There was no getting rid of it [the thought of his condition]. It was pressed upon me by every object within sight or hearing, animate or inanimate. The silver trump of freedom had roused my soul to eternal wakefulness. Freedom now appeared, to disappear no more forever. It was heard in every sound, and seen in everything. It was ever present to torment me with a sense of my wretched condition. I saw nothing without seeing it, I heard nothing without hearing it, and felt nothing without feeling it. It looked from every star; it smiled in every calm, breathed in every wind, and moved in every storm."—*Autobiography*, pp. 40, 41.

OUTLINE OF A MAN. 87

That was just *eleven years* ago,—and what is Frederick Douglass now? I would fain avoid the language of exaggeration. It is ever a cruel kindness which over-praises, exciting expectations, which cannot but be disappointed. But when, in view of the fact that the subject of this sketch was but thirteen years ago A SLAVE, in all the darkness and disability of Southern bondage, I affirm that his present character, attainments, and position constitute a phenomenon hitherto perhaps unprecedented in the history of intellectual and moral achievement, none who know and are competent to weigh the facts, will account the terms extravagant. It is not to be expected but that his mental condition should betray his early disadvantages. His information, though amazing, under the circumstances, will not of course bear comparison, in fulness and accuracy, with that of men who have been accumulating their resources from childhood. In his writings, the deficiency of early discipline is most manifest, rendering them diffuse and unequal, though always interesting, and often exceedingly effective. He is properly an *orator*. His addresses, like those of Whitfield, and many other popular speakers, lose a large proportion of their effect in reading. They require the living voice, and the magnetic presence of the orator. But even in this respect, Douglass is not uniform in his performance, but is quite dependent on his *surroundings*, and the inspiration of the moment. But when, all these consenting, he becomes thoroughly possessed of his theme, and his tall form—six feet high and straight as an arrow,—his bearing dignified and graceful,—self-possessed, yet modest,—his countenance flexible, and wonderful in power of expression, and his voice, with its rich and varied modulation, are all summoned to the work of enchantment, many a rapt assembly, insignificant in neither numbers nor intelligence, can testify to the witchery of his eloquence.

And, after all, the *moral* features of this interesting character constitute its principal charm. The integrity and manliness of Frederick Douglass, potent and acknowledged where he is at all known, have much to do with his influence as a popular orator. It has been customary, with a certain class of Shibboleth-pronouncers to class him with infidels, but this is only the appropriate and characteristic retort of a certain sort of "highly respectable" Christianity to his uncompromising denunciations of its hollow and selfish character. *I* think Frederick Douglass is a Christian; he is a gentleman, I *know*. There are few white men of my acquaintance, who could have borne so much adulation, without losing the balance of their self-appreciation. Nobody ever knew Frederick Douglass to over-rate himself, or to thrust himself anywhere where he did not belong, or upon anybody who might by any possibility object to his companionship,—unless, in the latter case, when he deemed necessary the assertion of a simple right. Whence he got his retiring and graceful modesty, and his nice sense of the minute proprieties,—unless it be somehow in his *blood*,—is a mystery to me. Can it be possible that such refinements are *scourged* into men "down South?" An illustration of this may be seen in his response to those gentlemen of Rochester, who, by way of gratifying a grudge against the Anti-slavery faction of their party, nominated Douglass for Congress in derision.

"Gentlemen:—I have learned with some surprise, that in the Whig Convention held in this city on Saturday last, you signified, by your votes, a desire to make me your representative in the Legislature of this State. Never having, at any time that I recollect, thought, spoken, or acted, in any way, to commit myself to either the principles or the policy of the Whig party; but on the contrary, having always held, and publicly expressed opinions diametrically opposed to those held by that part of the Whig party which you are supposed to represent, your voting for me, I am bound in courtesy to suppose, is founded in a misapprehension of my political sentiments.

"Lest you should, at any other time, commit a similar blunder, I beg to state, once for all, that I do not believe that the slavery question is settled, and settled forever. I do not believe that slave-catching is either a Christian duty, or an innocent amusement. I do not believe that he who breaks the arm of the kidnapper, or wrests the trembling captive from his grasp is 'a traitor.' I do not believe that Daniel Webster is the saviour of the Union, nor that the Union stands in need of such a saviour. I do not believe that human enactments are to be obeyed when they are point-blank against the law of the living God. And believing most fully, as I do, the reverse of all this, you will easily believe me to be a person wholly unfit to receive the suffrages of gentlemen holding the opinion and favoring the policy of that wing of the Whig party denominated 'the *Silver Grays.*'

"With all the respect which your derision permits me to entertain for you,

I am, gentlemen,
Your faithful fellow-citizen,
FREDERICK DOUGLASS."

The perpetrators of the wanton and gratuitous insult which elicited this beautiful rebuke, would be sadly outraged, were we to insist on withholding the title of "Gentlemen" from those who could, on any pretence, trample on the feelings of such as they esteem their inferiors. If they half begin to comprehend the meaning of the term, much more to feel its power, their cheeks must have crimsoned with shame, when they saw their own unprovoked assault, contrasted with the calm and self-respectful serenity of this reply.

Another instance of this dignity under circumstances of peculiar trial, may be found in his own account—in the columns of "Frederick Douglass' paper"—of a rencontre with a hotel clerk in Cleveland. It is as follows:

At the ringing of the morning bell for breakfast, I made my way to the table, supposing myself included in the call; but I was scarcely seated, when there stepped up to me a young man, apparently much agitated, saying: "Sir, you must leave this table." "And why," said I, "must I leave this table?" "I want no controversy with you. You must leave this table." I replied, "that I had regularly enrolled myself as a boarder in that house; I expected to pay the same charges imposed upon others; and I came to the table in obedience to the call of the bell; and if I left the table I must know the reason." "We will serve you in your room. It is against our rules." "You should have informed me of *your rules* earlier. Where are your rules? Let me see them." "I don't want any altercation with you. You must leave this table." "But have I not deported myself as a gentleman? What have I done?

Is there any gentleman who objects to my being seated here?" (There was silence round the table.) "Come, sir, come, sir, you must leave this table at once." "Well, sir, I cannot leave it unless you will give me a better reason than you have done for my removal." "Well, I'll give you a reason if you'll leave the table and go to another room." "That, sir, I will not do. You have invidiously selected me out of all this company, to be dragged from this table, and have thereby reflected upon me as a man and a gentleman; and the reason for this treatment shall be as public as the insult you have offered." At these remarks, my carrot-headed assailant left me, *as he said*, to get help to remove me from the table. Meanwhile I called upon one of the servants (who appeared to wait upon me with alacrity) to help me to a cup of coffee, and assisting myself to some of the good things before me, I quietly and thankfully partook of my morning meal without further annoyance.

Whatever may have been the duty of Mr. Douglass, (and none who know him can for a moment doubt what his inclination would have been,) in case the proscriptive "rules of the house" had been previously made known to him, the justice, as well as the gentlemanly self-possession of his bearing, in relation to this public outrage, must, I think, be sufficiently obvious.

****

Rev. Robt. R. Raymond

THE HEROIC SLAVE-WOMAN.

It was my privilege to see much of Edward S. Abdy, Esq., of England, during his visit to our country, in 1833 and 1834. The first time I met him was at the house of Mr. James Forten, of Philadelphia, in company with two other English gentlemen, who had come to the United States, commissioned by the British Parliament to examine our systems of prison and penitentiary discipline. Mr. Abdy was interested in whatsoever affected the welfare of man. But he was more particularly devoted to the investigation of slavery. He travelled extensively in our Southern States, and contemplated with his own eyes the manifold abominations of our American despotism. He was too much exasperated by our tyranny to be enamoured of our democratic institutions; and on his return to England, he published two very sensible volumes, that were so little complimentary to our nation, that our booksellers thought it not worth their while to republish them.

This warm-hearted philanthropist visited me several times at my home in Connecticut. The last afternoon that he was there, we were sitting together at my study window, when our attention was arrested by a very handsome carriage driving up to the hotel opposite my house. A gentleman and lady occupied the back seat; and on the front were two children tended by a black woman, who wore the turban, that was then more than now, usually worn by *slave* women.

We hastened over to the hotel, and soon entered into conversation with the slave-holder. He was polite, but somewhat nonchalant, and defiant of our sympathy with his victim. He readily acknowledged, as slave-holders of that day generally did, that, abstractly considered, the enslavement of fellow men was a great wrong; but then he contended that it had become a necessary evil, necessary to the enslaved, no less than to the enslavers; the former being unable to do without masters, as much as the latter were to do without servants. And he added, in a very confident tone, "you are at liberty to persuade our servant-woman to remain here, if you can."

Thus challenged, we of course sought an interview with the slave; and informed her that having been brought by her master into the free States, she was, by the laws of the land, set at liberty. "No, I am not, gentlemen," was her prompt reply. We adduced cases, and quoted authorities to establish our assertion that she was free. But she significantly shook her head, and still insisted that the examples and the legal decisions did not reach her case. "For," said she, "*I promised* mistress that I would go back with her and the children." Mr. Abdy undertook to argue with her that such a promise was not binding. He had been drilled in the moral philosophy of Dr. Paley, and in that debate seemed to be possessed of its spirit.

But he failed to make any visible impression upon the woman. She had bound herself by a promise to her mistress, that she would not leave her; and that promise had fastened upon her conscience an obligation, from which she could not be persuaded, that even her natural right to liberty could exonerate her. Mr. Abdy at last was impatient with her, and said, in his haste, "is it possible that you do not wish to be free?" She replied with solemn earnestness, "was there ever a slave that did not wish to be free? I long for liberty. I will get out of slavery, if I can, the day after I have returned, but go back I must, because I *promised* that I would." At this, we desisted from our endeavor to induce her to take the boon that was, apparently to us, within her reach. We could not but feel a profound respect for that moral sensibility which would not allow her to embrace even her freedom, at the expense of violating a promise.

The next morning, at an early hour, the slave-holder with his wife and children drove off, leaving the slave-woman and their heaviest trunk to be brought on after them in the stage-coach. We could not refrain from again trying to persuade her to remain and be free. We told her that her master had given us leave to persuade her if we could. She pointed to the trunk, and to a very valuable gold watch and chain, which her mistress had committed to her care, and insisted that fidelity to a trust was of more consequence to her soul even than the attainment of liberty. Mr. Abdy offered to take the trunk and watch into his charge, follow her master, and deliver them into his hands. But she could not be made to see that in this there would be no violation of her duty. And then her own person, that, too, she had promised should be returned to the home of her master; and much as she longed for liberty, she longed for a clear conscience more.

Mr. Abdy was astonished, delighted at this instance of heroice virtue in a poor, ignorant slave. He packed his trunk, gave me a hearty adieu, and, when the coach drove up, he took his seat on the outside with the trunk and the slave—chattels of a Mississippi slave-holder—that he might study for a few hours more the morality of that strong-hearted woman, who could not be bribed to violate her promise, even by the gift of liberty.

It was the last time I saw Mr. Abdy,—and it was a sight to be remembered,—he an accomplished English gentleman, a Fellow of Oxford or Cambridge University, riding on the driver's box of a stage-coach, side by side with an American slave-woman, that he might learn more of her history and character.

> "Full many a gem, of purest ray serene,
> The dark unfathomed caves of ocean bear;
> Full many a flower is born to blush unseen,
> And waste its sweetness on the desert air."

Yours, respectfully,

Samuel J. May

Rev. Samuel J. May

SYRACUSE, OCT. 9, 1852.

KOSSUTH.

You ask me what I think of Kossuth. The history of Kossuth is but partly told. An opinion of him now, is, of course, founded on the past and present. But so decisive have been the manifestations in regard to his abilities and aims, that we may confidently say he is the great man of the age. I don't mean that there is no other man who is responsible for as great or greater physical and intellectual endowments and education. We measure men by what they *do*, not by what they are *able* to do. He is great, because he has manifested great thoughts and corresponding deeds. In this regard he has no superior.

When I speak of Kossuth as *great*, I mean that the divine elements of power, wisdom, and goodness are so mixed in him, as to qualify him to embrace the largest interests, and attract the agencies to secure those interests. That his eye sees, and his heart feels, and his philanthropy embraces a larger area, and is acknowledged by a larger portion of the human family than any other living man. I do not say there are not men living whose hearts are as large, whose abilities are as great, and whose virtues are as exalted as Kossuth's. Men, too, whose great qualities under like contingencies would, and by future contingencies may, brighten into a glory as large as his. Nor would I say it does not often require as great, or even greater talents and virtues to accomplish deeds of humanity or patriotism on a theatre vastly less dazzling and imposing. It is not necessary to my argument to exclude such conclusions. When God decrees great events, he brings upon the stage and qualifies the human instrumentalities by which such events are accomplished; and that, too, at the very time they are needed. We don't know the future; but if we are to measure the present and the past in the life of Kossuth, leaving alone the shadows which coming events cast in the path of our hopes, we must rank Kossuth with the greatest, and if we couple his heart with his deeds, with the best of mankind.

I am aware that the opinion I here give of the great Magyar, is widely different from the opinions of some others for whom I have very high respect. Gerrit Smith honors Kossuth; but he honors him only as a patriot, a christian patriot. Professor Atler of McGranville College in an oration that does him credit as a philosopher and orator, says, that "he who thinks the largest thought is the ruler of the world,"—and yet he dwarfs the character of Kossuth to the simple patriot of Hungary. To my mind, these are strange conclusions. It is the greatest thoughts illustrated by corresponding action that denotes the ruler of the world. It is the external manifestation of the mighty spiritual that demonstrates the right to rule mankind. Apply that rule to Kossuth, and I maintain his right to the sceptre of the world.

The brotherhood of nations is an idea to which philanthropy only could give birth. Its home is in the hearts of all good men, and yet, until Kossuth came before the world, that idea had been esteemed so vast in its circumference, so out of the reach of means, so far beyond the grasp of present experience and possibility, that he would have been thought a fanatic or a fool who attempted it. He, indeed, by power strictly personal, not only seized upon it as a practical thought, and nobly argued it, but has actually and bravely entered upon the experiment, and forced it upon the conceptions of the world, and organized, not in our country only, but in Europe, plans and parties for its realization. Here is not only a great *thought*, but a great *deed*. To gather up the philanthropic minds or the patriot minds of the world to embrace such an enterprise as not only a dutiful but practicable scheme, is an achievement that leaves out of sight any other achievement of eighteen hundred years.

It is not the development of abstract principles in science, in philosophy, or in religion, that establishes the highest claim to the world's gratitude and admiration. It is the successful application of those principles to human life and conduct, the setting them to work to restore the world to the shape and aspect which God gave it, that demonstrates the God-like in man. It is the manifestation of a great idea upon the external, as God's great thoughts are manifested by the landscape, the ocean, and the heavens, by which we arrive at the spiritual power that conceived them. A patriot indeed! The great Hungarian *did* attempt to link America to his great purpose by appeals to her patriotism. It was the only common sentiment between our country and him. It is America's loftiest thought. Her beau-ideal of public virtue. I don't mean that there was no Christianity or philanthropy in the United States when Kossuth came amongst us; but I do mean that, as a nation, we had none of them. He came on an errand of practical philanthropy; to appeal to our national heart, and cause the only cord of humanity in it that could be touched, to vibrate in unison with his own in behalf of the down-trodden nations of the world. He wished to engage its organic power in behalf of national law. Had Kossuth appealed to any higher principle, he would have overshot his mark. Love of country is common, to the Christian and to the mere patriot. In the latter it is only selfishness, in the former genuine philanthropy. American patriotism was the only aperture through which he could reach our nation's heart, to raise it to the higher region of philanthropy, and place it in his own bosom, and impregnate it with his own holy sentiments, that their sympathies might circulate together for a common brotherhood. He represented Hungary. He appeared at our door as an outraged brother, to enlist us in behalf of a brother's rights and wrongs. He sought to excite in the nation's bosom the activity of a common principle, due at all times, and from nations no less than individuals. It is the core of Christianity, described in these words, "do unto others as you would have others do unto you."

Our Washington had told us "to cultivate peace with all nations, and form entangling alliances with none." Our sensual and short-sighted statesmen construed the sentiment as the rule of active power. Instead of adopting it as Washington probably intended it, as a rule of temporary policy, they inculcated the notion that we were to cut ourselves clear from the family of nations, and live only for ourselves. The large patriotism of Washington they had shrunken to the merest selfishness. We may well thank God for the providence which sent Kossuth among us, to relieve his fame from the suspicion of having begot, and our country from the sin of cherishing, so weak and dishonoring a delusion. Heaven-assisted man only could have dreamed of believing a nation so securely blinded. Like the prophet of God, whose lips were touched with celestial fire, he breathed upon the spell, and it vanished. The nation's eyes were opened. It saw, and all true men admitted, that the sentiment was designed and adapted only to our infancy, and, to use his own figure, no more fitting our manhood, than the clothes of an infant are fitting the full grown man.

Now I admit we had philanthropists, wise men, orators, and some statesmen, who asserted the doctrine of the human brotherhood, yet we had no Kossuth to dissolve (if I may so speak) this Washingtonian delusion. Kossuth touched it and it disappeared. The nation seemed to have come to a new birth. Its heart, like the rock in the desert which was touched by the staff of the prophet, opened, and its imprisoned waters poured over the world. We all felt as the bondman feels who is set free by a strong man. From that moment we grew larger, saw farther, and felt our hearts moving over an unlimited area of humanity. From that moment we felt that a new day was dawning. From that moment the principle of the human brotherhood struck its deep roots in our soil, as immovable as our mountains, as irradicable as our religion. Nor was it in America alone that this sentiment was then awakened. Touched by his notes, it trembled in the bosom of Europe. The heart of humanity throbbed with a common sympathy throughout the civilized world. Kossuth and Mazzini, crushed from beneath, ascended above the despotisms of the world in the clear upper sky, and, in sight of heaven and earth, reflected God's light and curse upon them; and called into being the activities which we hope is to tumble them in a common ruin, as the precursor of the holy compact which shall secure all human rights.

It is objected that Kossuth did not denounce our slavery. The same objection has equal strength against the philanthropy of Paul and Jesus. I shall not dwell on this point. He did denounce American slavery. The presence of Kossuth was a killing rebuke, his words a consuming fire to it. The former is still felt as an incurable wound, and the latter still scorches to the very centre of its vitality. I have it from high authority, when Kossuth first came upon the soil, and into the atmosphere of American slavery, his soul was so shocked and disgusted by its offensiveness, that he proposed to abandon his mission in those States where it existed, and denounce it specifically; and was only deterred from doing so, by his sense of the more comprehensive claims of that mission, which embraced the utter destruction of all human oppression. I drop this topic with the remark, that this objection, and all objections to his philanthropy, within my knowledge, were made antecedent to his inimitable speech in New York city, in behalf of his mother and sisters, a short time before he took his departure for Europe. If there is not Christianity, philanthropy, anti-slavery in that speech, we may despair of finding it in earth, or even in the heavens. I have never read anything so representative of heaven's mercy, or angels' eloquence, as that. Oh! I wish the world knew it by heart. Methinks if it did, all wrong and oppression would disappear from among men.

I was going to speak of the future, and of Mazzini, the twin apostle of liberty, whose exile was wrung from the heart of poor Italy. But the subject exceeds the brevity which must govern me. These rulers of the world are linked with the mighty events which are fast becoming history. From their hiding-places in London, they are moving and controlling the passions which seem ready to break forth and obliterate every cruel code under the sun, and hasten the time when all men shall feel as brethren, and mingle their hearts in anthems of gratitude and love.

John Thomas

Syracuse, Nov. 14, 1852.

THE HEROIC SLAVE.

PART I.

Oh! child of grief, why weepest thou?
Why droops thy sad and mournful brow?
Why is thy look so like despair?
What deep, sad sorrow lingers there?

THE State of Virginia is famous in American annals for the multitudinous array of her statesmen and heroes. She has been dignified by some the mother of statesmen. History has not been sparing in recording their names, or in blazoning their deeds. Her high position in this respect, has given her an enviable distinction among her sister States. With Virginia for his birth-place, even a man of ordinary parts, on account of the general partiality for her sons, easily rises to eminent stations. Men, not great enough to attract special attention in their native States, have, like a certain distinguished citizen in the State of New York, sighed and repined that they were not born in Virginia. Yet not all the great ones of the Old Dominion have, by the fact of their birth-place, escaped undeserved obscurity. By some strange neglect, *one* of the truest, manliest, and bravest of her children,—one who, in after years, will, I think, command the pen of genius to set his merits forth, holds now no higher place in the records of that grand old Commonwealth than is held by a horse or an ox. Let those account for it who can, but there stands the fact, that a man who loved liberty as well as did Patrick Henry,—who deserved it as much as Thomas Jefferson,—and who fought for it with a valor as high, an arm as strong, and against odds as great, as he who led all the armies of the American colonies through the great war for freedom and independence, lives now only in the chattel records of his native State.

Glimpses of this great character are all that can now be presented. He is brought to view only by a few transient incidents, and these afford but partial satisfaction. Like a guiding star on a stormy night, he is seen through the parted clouds and the howling tempests; or, like the gray peak of a menacing rock on a perilous coast, he is seen by the quivering flash of angry lightning, and he again disappears covered with mystery.

Curiously, earnestly, anxiously we peer into the dark, and wish even for the blinding flash, or the light of northern skies to reveal him. But alas! he is still enveloped in darkness, and we return from the pursuit like a wearied and disheartened mother, (after a tedious and unsuccessful search for a lost child,) who returns weighed down with disappointment and sorrow. Speaking of marks, traces, possibles, and probabilities, we come before our readers.

In the spring of 1835, on a Sabbath morning, within hearing of the solemn peals of the church bells at a distant village, a Northern traveller through the State of Virginia drew up his horse to drink at a sparkling brook, near the edge of a dark pine forest. While his weary and thirsty steed drew in the grateful water, the rider caught the sound of a human voice, apparently engaged in earnest conversation.

Following the direction of the sound, he descried, among the tall pines, the man whose voice had arrested his attention. "To whom can he be speaking?" thought the traveller. "He seems to be alone." The circumstance interested him much, and he became intensely curious to know what thoughts and feelings, or, it might be, high aspirations, guided those rich and mellow accents. Tieing his horse at a short distance from the brook, he stealthily drew near the solitary speaker; and, concealing himself by the side of a huge fallen tree, he distinctly heard the following soliloquy:—

"What, then, is life to me? it is aimless and worthless, and worse than worthless. Those birds, perched on yon swinging boughs, in friendly conclave, sounding forth their merry notes in seeming worship of the rising sun, though liable to the sportsman's fowling-piece, are still my superiors. They *live free*, though they may die slaves. They fly where they list by day, and retire in freedom at night. But what is freedom to me, or I to it? I am a *slave*,—born a slave, an abject slave,—even before I made part of this breathing world, the scourge was platted for my back; the fetters were forged for my limbs. How mean a thing am I. That accursed and crawling snake, that miserable reptile, that has just glided into its slimy home, is freer and better off than I. He escaped my blow, and is safe. But here am I, a man,—yes, *a man!*—with thoughts and wishes, with powers and faculties as far as angel's flight above that hated reptile,—yet he is my superior, and scorns to own me as his master, or to stop to take my blows. When he saw my uplifted arm, he darted beyond my reach, and turned to give me battle. I dare not do as much as that. I neither run nor fight, but do meanly stand, answering each heavy blow of a cruel master with doleful wails and piteous cries. I am galled with irons; but even these are more tolerable than the consciousness, the *galling* consciousness of cowardice and indecision. Can it be that I *dare* not run away? *Perish the thought*, I *dare* do any thing which may be done by another. When that young man struggled with the waves *for life*, and others stood back appalled in helpless horror, did I not plunge in, forgetful of life, to save his? The raging bull from whom all others fled, pale with fright, did I not keep at bay with a single pitch-fork? Could a coward do that? *No,—no,*—I wrong myself,—I am no coward. *Liberty* I will have, or die in the attempt to gain it. This working that others may live in idleness! This cringing submission to insolence and curses! This living under the constant dread and apprehension of being sold and transferred, like a mere brute, is *too* much for me. I will stand it no longer. What others have done, I will do. These trusty legs, or these sinewy arms shall place me among the free. Tom escaped; so can I. The North Star will not be less kind to me than to him. I will follow it. I will at least make the trial. I have nothing to lose. If I am caught, I shall only be a slave. If I am shot, I shall only lose a life which is a burden and a curse. If I get clear, (as something tells me I

THE HEROIC SLAVE.

shall,) liberty, the inalienable birth-right of every man, precious and priceless, will be mine. My resolution is fixed. *I shall be free.*"

At these words the traveller raised his head cautiously and noiselessly, and caught, from his hiding-place, a full view of the unsuspecting speaker. Madison (for that was the name of our hero) was standing erect, a smile of satisfaction rippled upon his expressive countenance, like that which plays upon the face of one who has but just solved a difficult problem, or vanquished a malignant foe; for at that moment he was free, at least in spirit. The future gleamed brightly before him, and his fetters lay broken at his feet. His air was triumphant.

Madison was of manly form. Tall, symmetrical, round, and strong. In his movements he seemed to combine, with the strength of the lion, a lion's elasticity. His torn sleeves disclosed arms like polished iron. His face was "black, but comely." His eye, lit with emotion, kept guard under a brow as dark and as glossy as the raven's wing. His whole appearance betokened Herculean strength; yet there was nothing savage or forbidding in his aspect. A child might play in his arms, or dance on his shoulders. A giant's strength, but not a giant's heart was in him. His broad mouth and nose spoke only of good mature and kindness. But his voice, that unfailing index of the soul, though full and melodious, had that in it which could terrify as well as charm. He was just the man you would choose when hardships were to be endured, or danger to be encountered,—intelligent and brave. He had the head to conceive, and the hand to execute. In a word, he was one to be sought as a friend, but to be dreaded as an enemy.

As our traveller gazed upon him, he almost trembled at the thought of his dangerous intrusion. Still he could not quit the place. He had long desired to sound the mysterious depths of the thoughts and feelings of a slave. He was not, therefore, disposed to allow so providential an opportunity to pass unimproved. He resolved to hear more; so he listened again for those mellow and mournful accents which, he says, made such an impression upon him as can never be erased. He did not have to wait long. There came another gush from the same full fountain; now bitter, and now sweet. Scathing denunciations of the cruelty and injustice of slavery; heart-touching narrations of his own personal suffering, intermingled with prayers to the God of the oppressed for help and deliverance, were followed by presentations of the dangers and difficulties of escape, and formed the burden of his eloquent utterances; but his high resolution clung to him,—for he ended each speech by an emphatic declaration of his purpose to be free. It seemed that the very repetition of this, imparted a glow to his countenance. The hope of freedom seemed to sweeten, for a season, the bitter cup of slavery, and to make it, for a time, tolerable; for when in the very whirlwind of anguish,—when his heart's cord seemed screwed up to snapping tension, hope sprung up and soothed his troubled spirit. Fitfully he would exclaim, "How can I leave her? Poor thing! what can she do when I am gone? Oh! oh! 'tis impossible that I can leave poor Susan!"

A brief pause intervened. Our traveller raised his head, and saw again the sorrow-smitten slave. His eye was fixed upon the ground. The strong man staggered under a heavy load. Recovering himself, he argued thus aloud: "All is uncertain here. To-morrow's sun may not rise before I am sold, and separated from her I love. What, then, could I do for her? I should be in more hopeless slavery, and she no nearer to liberty, — whereas if I were free, — my arms my own, — I might devise the means to rescue her."

This said, Madison cast around a searching glance, as if the thought of being overheard had flashed across his mind. He said no more, but, with measured steps, walked away, and was lost to the eye of our traveller amidst the wildering woods.

Long after Madison had left the ground, Mr. Listwell (our traveller) remained in motionless silence, meditating on the extraordinary revelations to which he had listened. He seemed fastened to the spot, and stood half hoping, half fearing the return of the sable preacher to his solitary temple. The speech of Madison rung through the chambers of his soul, and vibrated through his entire frame. "Here is indeed a man," thought he, "of rare endowments, — a child of God, — guilty of no crime but the color of his skin, — hiding away from the face of humanity, and pouring out his thoughts and feelings, his hopes and resolutions to the lonely woods; to him those distant church bells have no grateful music. He shuns the church, the altar, and the great congregation of christian worshippers, and wanders away to the gloomy forest, to utter in the vacant air complaints and griefs, which the religion of his times and his country can neither console nor relieve. Goaded almost to madness by the sense of the injustice done him, he resorts hither to give vent to his pent up feelings, and to debate with himself the feasibility of plans, plans of his own invention, for his own deliverance. From this hour I am an abolitionist. I have seen enough and heard enough, and I shall go to my home in Ohio resolved to atone for my past indifference to this ill-starred race, by making such exertions as I shall be able to do, for the speedy emancipation of every slave in the land."

PART II.

"The gaudy, blabbling and remorseful day
Is crept into the bosom of the sea;
And now loud-howling wolves arouse the jades
That drag the tragic melancholy night;
Who with their drowsy, slow, and flagging wings
Clip dead men's graves, and from their misty jaws
Breathe foul contagions, darkness in the air."

Shakspeare.

Five years after the foregoing singular occurrence, in the winter of 1840, Mr. and Mrs. Listwell sat together by the fireside of their own happy home, in the State of Ohio. The children were all gone to bed. A single lamp burnt brightly on the centre-table. All was still and comfortable within; but the night was cold and dark; a heavy wind sighed and moaned sorrowfully around the house and barn, occasionally bringing against the clattering windows a stray leaf from the large oak trees that embowered their dwelling. It was a night for strange noises and for strange fancies. A whole wilderness of thought might pass through one's mind during such an evening. The smouldering embers, partaking of the spirit of the restless night, became fruitful of varied and fantastic pictures, and revived many bygone scenes and old impressions. The happy pair seemed to sit in silent fascination, gazing on the fire. Suddenly this *reverie* was interrupted by a heavy growl. Ordinarily such an occurrence would have scarcely provoked a single word, or excited the least apprehension. But there are certain seasons when the slightest sound sends a jar through all the subtle chambers of the mind; and such a season was this. The happy pair started up, as if some sudden danger had come upon them. The growl was from their trusty watch-dog.

"What can it mean? certainly no one can be out on such a night as this," said Mrs. Listwell.

"The wind has deceived the dog, my dear; he has mistaken the noise of falling branches, brought down by the wind, for that of the footsteps of persons coming to the house. I have several times to-night thought that I heard the sound of footsteps. I am sure, however, that it was but the wind. Friends would not be likely to come out at such an hour, or such a night; and thieves are too lazy and self-indulgent to expose themselves to this biting frost; but should there be any one about, our brave old Monte, who is on the look-out, will not be slow in sounding the alarm."

Saying this they quietly left the window, whither they had gone to learn the cause of the menacing growl, and re-seated themselves by the fire, as if reluctant to leave the slowly expiring embers, although the hour was late. A few minutes only intervened after resuming their seats, when again their sober meditations were disturbed. Their faithful dog now growled and barked furiously, as if assailed by an advancing foe. Simultaneously the good couple arose, and stood in mute expectation. The contest without seemed fierce and violent. It was, however, soon over,—the barking ceased, for, with true canine instinct, Monte quickly discovered that a friend, not an enemy of the family, was coming to the house, and instead of rushing to repel the supposed intruder, he was now at the door, whimpering and dancing for the admission of himself and his newly made friend.

Mr. Listwell knew by this movement that all was well; he advanced and opened the door, and saw by the light that streamed out into the darkness, a tall man advancing slowly towards the house, with a stick in one hand, and a small bundle in the other. "It is a traveller," thought he, "who has missed his way, and is coming to inquire the road. I am glad we did not go to bed earlier,—I have felt all the evening as if somebody would be here to-night."

The man had now halted a short distance from the door, and looked prepared alike for flight or battle. "Come in, sir, don't be alarmed, you have probably lost your way."

Slightly hesitating, the traveller walked in; not, however, without regarding his host with a scrutinizing glance. "No, sir," said he, "I have come to ask you a greater favor."

Instantly Mr. Listwell exclaimed, (as the recollection of the Virginia forest scene flashed upon him,) "Oh, sir, I know not your name, but I have seen your face, and heard your voice before. I am glad to see you. *I know all.* You are flying for your liberty,—be seated,—be seated,—banish all fear. You are safe under my roof."

This recognition, so unexpected, rather disconcerted and disquieted the noble fugitive. The timidity and suspicion of persons escaping from slavery are easily awakened, and often what is intended to dispel the one, and to allay the other, has precisely the opposite effect. It was so in this case. Quickly observing the unhappy impression made by his words and action, Mr. Listwell assumed a more quiet and inquiring aspect, and finally succeeded in removing the apprehensions which his very natural and generous salutation had aroused.

Thus assured, the stranger said, "Sir, you have rightly guessed, I am, indeed, a fugitive from slavery. My name is Madison,—Madison Washington my mother used to call me. I am on my way to Canada, where I learn that persons of my color are protected in all the rights of men; and my object in calling upon you was, to beg the privilege of resting my weary limbs for the night in your barn. It was my purpose to have continued my journey till morning; but the piercing cold, and the frowning darkness compelled me to seek shelter; and, seeing a light through the lattice of your window, I was encouraged to come here to beg the privilege named. You will do me a great favor by affording me shelter for the night."

"A resting-place, indeed, sir, you shall have; not, however, in my barn, but in the best room of my house. Consider yourself, if you please, under the roof of a friend; for such I am to you, and to all your deeply injured race."

While this introductory conversation was going on, the kind lady had revived the fire, and was diligently preparing supper; for she, not less than her husband, felt for the sorrows of the oppressed and hunted ones of earth, and was always glad of an opportunity to do them a service. A bountiful repast was quickly prepared, and the hungry and toil-worn bondman was cordially invited to partake thereof. Gratefully he acknowledged the favor of his benevolent benefactress; but appeared scarcely to understand what such hospitality could mean. It was the first time in his life that he had met so humane and friendly a greeting at the hands of persons whose color was unlike his own; yet it was impossible for him to doubt the charitableness of his new friends, or the genuineness of the welcome so freely given; and he therefore, with many thanks, took his seat at the table with Mr. and Mrs. Listwell, who, desirous to make him feel at home, took a cup of tea themselves, while urging upon Madison the best that the house could afford.

Supper over, all doubts and apprehensions banished, the three drew around the blazing fire, and a conversation commenced which lasted till long after midnight.

"Now," said Madison to Mr. Listwell, "I was a little surprised and alarmed when I came in, by what you said; do tell me, sir, *why* you thought you had seen my face before, and by what you knew me to be a fugitive from slavery; for I am sure that I never was before in this neighborhood, and I certainly sought to conceal what I supposed to be the manner of a fugitive slave."

Mr. Listwell at once frankly disclosed the secret; describing the place where he first saw him; rehearsing the language which he (Madison) had used; referring to the effect which his manner and speech had made upon him; declaring the resolution he there formed to be an abolitionist; telling how often he had spoken of the circumstance, and the deep concern he had ever since felt to know what had become of him; and whether he had carried out the purpose to make his escape, as in the woods he declared he would do.

"Ever since that morning," said Mr. Listwell, "you have seldom been absent from my mind, and though now I did not dare to hope that I should ever see you again, I have often wished that such might be my fortune; for, from that hour, your face seemed to be daguerreotyped on my memory."

Madison looked quite astonished, and felt amazed at the narration to which he had listened. After recovering himself he said, "I well remember that morning, and the bitter anguish that wrung my heart; I will state the occasion of it. I had, on the previous Saturday, suffered a cruel lashing; had been tied up to the limb of a tree, with my feet chained together, and a heavy iron bar placed between my ankles. Thus suspended, I received on my naked back forty stripes, and was kept in this distressing position three or four hours, and was then let down, only to have my torture increased; for my bleeding back, gashed by the cow-skin, was washed by the overseer with old brine, partly to augment my suffering, and partly, as he said, to prevent inflammation. My crime was that I had stayed longer at the mill, the day previous, than it was thought I ought to have done, which, I assured my master and the overseer, was no fault of mine; but no excuses were allowed. 'Hold your tongue, you impudent rascal,' met my every explanation. Slave-holders are so imperious when their passions are excited, as to construe every word of the slave into insolence. I could do nothing but submit to the agonizing infliction. Smarting still from the wounds, as well as from the consciousness of being whipt for no cause, I took advantage of the absence of my master, who had gone to church, to spend the time in the woods, and brood over my wretched lot. Oh, sir, I remember it well,—and can never forget it."

"But this was five years ago; where have you been since?"

"I will try to tell you," said Madison. "Just four weeks after that Sabbath morning, I gathered up the few rags of clothing I had, and started, as I supposed, for the North and for freedom. I must not stop to describe my feelings on taking this step. It seemed like taking a leap into the dark. The thought of leaving my poor wife and two little children caused me indescribable anguish; but consoling myself with the reflection that once free, I could, possibly, devise ways and means to gain their freedom also, I nerved myself up to make the attempt. I started, but ill-luck attended me; for after being out a whole week, strange to say, I still found myself on my master's grounds; the third night after being out, a season of clouds and rain set in, wholly preventing me from seeing the North Star, which I had trusted as my guide, not dreaming that clouds might intervene between us.

"This circumstance was fatal to my project, for in losing my star, I lost my way; so when I supposed I was far towards the North, and had almost gained my freedom, I discovered myself at the very point from which I had started. It was a severe trial, for I arrived at home in great destitution; my feet were sore, and in travelling in the dark, I had dashed my foot against a stump, and started a nail, and lamed myself. I was wet and cold; one week had exhausted all my stores; and when I landed on my master's plantation, with all my work to do over again,—hungry, tired, lame, and bewildered,—I almost cursed the day that I was born. In this extremity I approached the quarters. I did so stealthily, although in my desperation I hardly cared whether I was discovered or not. Peeping through the rents of the quarters, I saw my fellow-slaves seated by a warm fire, merrily passing away the time, as though their hearts knew no sorrow. Although I envied their seeming contentment, all wretched as I was, I despised the cowardly acquiescence in their own degradation which it implied, and felt a kind of pride and glory in my own desperate lot. I dared not enter the quarters,—for where there is seeming contentment with slavery, there is certain treachery to freedom. I proceeded towards the great house, in the hope of catching a glimpse of my poor wife, whom I knew might be trusted with my secrets even on the scaffold. Just as I reached the fence which divided the field from the garden, I saw a woman in the yard, who in the darkness I took to be my wife; but a nearer approach told me it was not she. I was about to speak; had I done so, I would not have been here this night; for an alarm would have been sounded, and the hunters been put on my track. Here were hunger, cold, thirst, disappointment, and chagrin, confronted only by the dim hope of liberty. I tremble to think of that dreadful hour. To face the deadly cannon's mouth in warm blood unterrified, is, I think, a small achievement, compared with a conflict like this with gaunt starvation. The gnawings of hunger conquers by degrees, till all that a man has he would give in exchange for a single crust of bread. Thank God, I was not quite reduced to this extremity.

"Happily for me, before the fatal moment of utter despair, my good wife made her appearance in the yard. It was she; I knew her step. All was well now. I was, however, afraid to speak, lest I should frighten her. Yet speak I did; and, to my great joy, my voice was known. Our meeting can be more easily imagined than described. For a time hunger, thirst, weariness, and lameness were forgotten. But it was soon necessary for her to return to the house. She being a house-servant, her absence from the kitchen, if discovered, might have excited suspicion. Our parting was like tearing the flesh from my bones; yet it was the part of wisdom for her to go. She left me with the purpose of meeting me at midnight in the very forest where you last saw me. She knew the place well, as one of my melancholy resorts, and could easily find it, though the night was dark.

"I hastened away, therefore, and concealed myself, to await the arrival of my good angel. As I lay there among the leaves, I was strongly tempted to return again to the house of my master and give myself up; but remembering my solemn pledge on that memorable Sunday morning, I was able to linger out the two long hours between ten and midnight. I may well call them long hours. I have endured much hardship; I have encountered many perils; but the anxiety of those two hours, was the bitterest I ever experienced. True to her word, my wife came laden with provisions, and we sat down on the side of a log, at that dark and lonesome hour of the night. I cannot say we talked; our feelings were too great for that; yet we came to an understanding that I should make the woods my home, for if I gave myself up, I should be whipped and sold away; and if I started for the North,

I should leave a wife doubly dear to me. We mutually determined, therefore, that I should remain in the vicinity. In the dismal swamps I lived, sir, five long years,—a cave for my home during the day. I wandered about at night with the wolf and the bear,—sustained by the promise that my good Susan would meet me in the pine woods at least once a week. This promise was redeemed, I assure you, to the letter, greatly to my relief. I had partly become contented with my mode of life, and had made up my mind to spend my days there; but the wilderness that sheltered me thus long took fire, and refused longer to be my hiding-place.

"I will not harrow up your feelings by portraying the terrific scene of this awful conflagration. There is nothing to which I can liken it. It was horribly and indescribably grand. The whole world seemed on fire, and it appeared to me that the day of judgment had come; that the burning bowels of the earth had burst forth, and that the end of all things was at hand. Bears and wolves, scorched from their mysterious hiding-places in the earth, and all the wild inhabitants of the untrodden forest, filled with a common dismay, ran forth, yelling, howling, bewildered amidst the smoke and flame. The very heavens seemed to rain down fire through the towering trees; it was by the merest chance that I escaped the devouring element. Running before it, and stopping occasionally to take breath, I looked back to behold its frightful ravages, and to drink in its savage magnificence. It was awful, thrilling, solemn, beyond compare. When aided by the fitful wind, the merciless tempest of fire swept on, sparkling, creaking, cracking, curling, roaring, out-doing in its dreadful splendor a thousand thunderstorms at once. From tree to tree it leaped, swallowing them up in its lurid, baleful glare; and leaving them leafless, limbless, charred, and lifeless behind. The scene was overwhelming, stunning,—nothing was spared,—cattle, tame and wild, herds of swine and of deer, wild beasts of every name and kind,—huge night-birds, bats, and owls, that had retired to their homes in lofty tree-tops to rest, perished in that fiery storm. The long-winged buzzard and croaking raven mingled their dismal cries with those of the countless myriads of small birds that rose up to the skies, and were lost to the sight in clouds of smoke and flame. Oh, I shudder when I think of it! Many a poor wandering fugitive, who, like myself, had sought among wild beasts the mercy denied by our fellow men, saw, in helpless consternation, his dwelling-place and city of refuge reduced to ashes forever. It was this grand conflagration that drove me hither; I ran alike from fire and from slavery."

After a slight pause, (for both speaker and hearers were deeply moved by the above recital,) Mr. Listwell, addressing Madison, said, "If it does not weary you too much, do tell us something of your journeyings since this disastrous burning,—we are deeply interested in everything which can throw light on the hardships of persons escaping from slavery; we could hear you talk all night; are there no incidents that you could relate of your travels hither? or are they such that you do not like to mention them."

"For the most part, sir, my course has been uninterrupted; and, considering the circumstances, at times even pleasant. I have suffered little for want of food; but I need not tell you how I got it. Your moral code may differ from mine, as your customs and usages are different. The fact is, sir, during my flight, I felt myself robbed by society of all my just rights; that I was in an enemy's land, who sought both my life and my liberty. They had transformed me into a brute; made merchandise of my body, and, for all the purposes of my flight, turned day into night,—and guided by my own necessities, and in contempt of their conventionalities, I did not scruple to take bread where I could get it."

"And just there you were right," said Mr. Listwell; "I once had doubts on this point myself, but a conversation with Gerrit Smith, (a man, by the way, that I wish you could see, for he is a devoted friend of your race, and I know he would receive you gladly,) put an end to all my doubts on this point. But do not let me interrupt you."

"I had but one narrow escape during my whole journey," said Madison.

"Do let us hear of it," said Mr. Listwell.

"Two weeks ago," continued Madison, "after travelling all night, I was overtaken by daybreak, in what seemed to me an almost interminable wood. I deemed it unsafe to go farther, and, as usual, I looked around for a suitable tree in which to spend the day. I liked one with a bushy top, and found one just to my mind. Up I climbed, and hiding myself as well as I could, I, with this strap, (pulling one out of his old coat-pocket,) lashed myself to a bough, and flattered myself that I should get a *good night's* sleep that day; but in this I was soon disappointed. I had scarcely got fastened to my natural hammock, when I heard the voices of a number of persons, apparently approaching the part of the woods where I was. Upon my word, sir, I dreaded more these human voices than I should have done those of wild beasts. I was at a loss to know what to do. If I descended, I should probably be discovered by the men; and if they had dogs I should, doubtless, be '*treed.*' It was an anxious moment, but hardships and dangers have been the accompaniments of my life; and have, perhaps, imparted to me a certain hardness of character, which, to some extent, adapts me to them. In my present predicament, I decided to hold my place in the tree-top, and abide the consequences. But here I must disappoint you; for the men, who were all colored, halted at least a hundred yards from me, and began with their axes, in right good earnest, to attack the trees. The sound of their laughing axes was like the report of as many well-charged pistols. By and by there came down at least a dozen trees with a terrible crash. They leaped upon the fallen trees with an air of victory. I could see no dog with them, and felt myself comparatively safe, though I could not forget the possibility that some freak or fancy might bring the axe a little nearer my dwelling than comported with my safety.

"There was no sleep for me that day, and I wished for night. You may imagine that the thought of having the tree attacked under me was far from agreeable, and that it very easily kept me on the look-out. The day was not without diversion. The men at work seemed to be a gay set; and they would often make the woods resound with that uncontrolled laughter for which we, as a race, are remarkable. I held my place in the tree till sunset,—saw the men put on their jackets to be off. I observed that all left the ground except one, whom I saw sitting on the side of a stump, with his head bowed, and his eyes apparently fixed on the ground. I became interested in him. After sitting in the position to which I have alluded ten or fifteen minutes, he left the stump, walked directly towards the tree in which I was secreted, and halted almost under the same. He stood for a moment and looked around, deliberately and reverently took off his hat, by which I saw that he was a man in the evening of life, slightly bald and quite gray. After laying down his hat carefully, he knelt and prayed aloud, and such a prayer, the most fervent, earnest, and solemn, to which I think I ever listened. After reverently addressing the Almighty, as the all-wise, all-good, and the common Father of all mankind, he besought God for grace, for strength, to bear up under, and to endure, as a good soldier, all the hardships and trials which beset the journey of life, and to enable him to live in a manner which accorded with the gospel of Christ. His soul now broke out in humble supplication for deliverance from bondage. 'O thou,' said he, 'that hearest the raven's cry, take pity on poor me! O deliver me! O deliver me! in mercy, O God, deliver me from the chains and manifold hardships of slavery! With thee, O Father, all things are possible. Thou canst stand and measure the earth. Thou hast beheld and drove asunder the nations,—all power is in thy hand,—thou didst say of old, "I have seen the affliction of my people, and am come to deliver them,"—Oh look down upon our afflictions, and have mercy upon us.' But I cannot repeat his prayer, nor can I give you an idea of its deep pathos. I had given but little attention to religion, and had but little faith in it; yet, as the old man prayed, I felt almost like coming down and kneel by his side, and mingle my broken complaint with his.

"He had already gained my confidence; as how could it be otherwise? I knew enough of religion to know that the man who prays in secret is far more likely to be sincere than he who loves to pray standing in the street, or in the great congregation. When he arose from his knees, like another Zacheus, I came down from the tree. He seemed a little alarmed at first, but I told him my story, and the good man embraced me in his arms, and assured me of his sympathy.

"I was now about out of provisions, and thought I might safely ask him to help me replenish my store. He said he had no money; but if he had, he would freely give it me. I told him I had *one dollar*; it was all the money I had in the world. I gave it to him, and asked him to purchase some crackers and cheese, and to kindly bring me the balance; that I would remain in or near that place, and would come to him on his return, if he would whistle. He was gone only about an hour. Meanwhile, from some cause or other, I know not what, (but as you shall see very wisely,) I changed my place. On his return I started to meet him; but it seemed as if the shadow of approaching danger fell upon my spirit, and checked my progress. In a very few minutes, closely on the heels of the old man, I distinctly saw *fourteen men*, with something like guns in their hands."

"Oh! the old wretch!" exclaimed Mrs. Listwell, "he had betrayed you, had he?"

"I think not," said Madison, "I cannot believe that the old man was to blame. He probably went into a store, asked for the articles for which I sent, and presented the bill I gave him; and it is so unusual for slaves in the country to have money, that fact, doubtless, excited suspicion, and gave rise to inquiry. I can easily believe that the truthfulness of the old man's character compelled him to disclose the facts; and thus were these blood-thirsty men put on my track. Of course I did not present myself; but hugged my hiding-place securely. If discovered and attacked, I resolved to sell my life as dearly as possible.

"After searching about the woods silently for a time, the whole company gathered around the old man; one charged him with lying, and called him an old villain; said he was a thief; charged him with stealing money; said if he did not instantly tell where he got it, they would take the shirt from his old back, and give him thirty-nine lashes.

"'I did *not* steal the money,' said the old man, 'it was given me, as I told you at the store; and if the man who gave it me is not here, it is not my fault.'

"'Hush! you lying old rascal; we'll make you smart for it. You shall not leave this spot until you have told where you got that money.'

"They now took hold of him, and began to strip him; while others went to get sticks with which to beat him. I felt, at the moment, like rushing out in the midst of them; but considering that the old man would be whipped the more for having aided a fugitive slave, and that, perhaps, in the *melée* he might be killed outright, I disobeyed this impulse. They tied him to a tree, and began to whip him. My own flesh crept at every blow, and I seem to hear the old man's piteous cries even now. They laid thirty-nine lashes on his bare back, and were going to repeat that number, when one of the company besought his comrades to desist. 'You'll kill the d—d old scoundrel! You've already whipt a dollar's worth out of him, even if he stole it!' 'O yes,' said another, 'let him down. He'll never tell us another lie, I'll warrant ye!' With this, one of the company untied the old man, and bid him go about his business.

The old man left, but the company remained as much as an hour, scouring the woods. Round and round they went, turning up the underbrush, and peering about like so many bloodhounds. Two or three times they came within six feet of where I lay. I tell you I held my stick with a firmer grasp than I did in coming up to your house to-night. I expected to level one of them at least. Fortunately, however, I eluded their pursuit, and they left me alone in the woods.

"My last dollar was now gone, and you may well suppose I felt the loss of it; but the thought of being once again free to pursue my journey, prevented that depression which a sense of destitution causes; so swinging my little bundle on my back, I caught a glimpse of the *Great Bear* (which ever points the way to my beloved star,) and I started again on my journey. What I lost in money I made up at a hen-roost that same night, upon which I fortunately came."

"But you didn't eat your food raw? How did you cook it?" said Mrs. Listwell.

"O no, Madam," said Madison, turning to his little bundle;—"I had the means of cooking." Here he took out of his bundle an old-fashioned tinder-box, and taking up a piece of a file, which he brought with him, he struck it with a heavy flint, and brought out at least a dozen sparks at once. "I have had this old box," said he, "more than five years. It is the *only* property saved from the fire in the dismal swamp. It has done me good service. It has given me the means of broiling many a chicken!"

It seemed quite a relief to Mrs. Listwell to know that Madison had, at least, lived upon cooked food. Women have a perfect horror of eating uncooked food.

By this time thoughts of what was best to be done about getting Madison to Canada, began to trouble Mr. Listwell; for the laws of Ohio were very stringent against any one who should aid, or who were found aiding a slave to escape through that State. A citizen, for the simple act of taking a fugitive slave in his carriage, had just been stripped of all his property, and thrown penniless upon the world. Notwithstanding this, Mr. Listwell was determined to see Madison safely on his way to Canada. "Give yourself no uneasiness," said he to Madison, "for if it cost my farm, I shall see you safely out of the States, and on your way to a land of liberty. Thank God that there is *such* a land so near us! You will spend to-morrow with us, and to-morrow night I will take you in my carriage to the Lake. Once upon that, and you are safe."

"Thank you! thank you," said the fugitive; "I will commit myself to your care."

For the *first* time during *five* years, Madison enjoyed the luxury of resting his limbs on a comfortable bed, and inside a human habitation. Looking at the white sheets, he said to Mr. Listwell, "What, sir! you don't mean that I shall sleep in that bed?"

"Oh yes, oh yes."

After Mr. Listwell left the room, Madison said he really hesitated whether or not he should lie on the floor; for that was *far* more comfortable and inviting than any bed to which he had been used.

We pass over the thoughts and feelings, the hopes and fears, the plans and purposes, that revolved in the mind of Madison during the day that he was secreted at the house of Mr. Listwell. The reader will be content to know that nothing occurred to endanger his liberty, or to excite alarm. Many were the little attentions bestowed upon him in his quiet retreat and hiding-place. In the evening, Mr. Listwell, after treating Madison to a new suit of winter clothes, and replenishing his exhausted purse with five dollars, all in silver, brought out his two-horse wagon, well provided with buffaloes, and silently started off with him to Cleveland. They arrived there without interruption, a few minutes before sunrise the next morning. Fortunately the steamer Admiral lay at the wharf, and was to start for Canada at nine o'clock. Here the last anticipated danger was surmounted. It was feared that just at this point the hunters of men might be on the look-out, and, possibly, pounce upon their victim. Mr. Listwell saw the captain of the boat; cautiously sounded him on the matter of carrying liberty-loving passengers, before he introduced his precious charge. This done, Madison was conducted on board. With usual generosity this true subject of the emancipating queen welcomed Madison, and assured him that he should be safely landed in Canada, free of charge. Madison now felt himself no more a piece of merchandise, but a passenger, and, like any other passenger, going about his business, carrying with him what belonged to him, and nothing which rightfully belonged to anybody else.

Wrapped in his new winter suit, snug and comfortable, a pocket full of silver, safe from his pursuers, embarked for a free country, Madison gave every sign of sincere gratitude, and bade his kind benefactor farewell, with such a grip of the hand as bespoke a heart full of honest manliness, and a soul that knew how to appreciate kindness. It need scarcely be said that Mr. Listwell was deeply moved by the gratitude and friendship he had excited in a nature so noble as that of the fugitive. He went to his home that day with a joy and gratification which knew no bounds. He had done something "to deliver the spoiled out of the hands of the spoiler," he had given bread to the hungry, and clothes to the naked; he had befriended a man to whom the laws of his country forbade all friendship,—and in proportion to the odds against his righteous deed, was the delightful satisfaction that gladdened his heart. On reaching home, he exclaimed, *"He is safe,—he is safe,—he is safe,"*—and the cup of his joy was shared by his excellent lady. The following letter was received from Madison a few days after.

"WINDSOR, CANADA WEST, DEC. 16, 1840.

My dear Friend,—for such you truly are:—

Madison is out of the woods at last; I nestle in the mane of the British lion, protected by his mighty paw from the talons and the beak of the American eagle. I AM FREE, and breathe an atmosphere too pure for *slaves*, slave-hunters, or slave-holders. My heart is full. As many thanks to you, sir, and to your kind lady, as there are pebbles on the shores of Lake Erie; and may the blessing of God rest upon you both. You will never be forgotten by your profoundly grateful friend,

MADISON WASHINGTON."

PART III.

— —His head was with his heart,
And that was far away!

Childe Harold.

Just upon the edge of the great road from Petersburg, Virginia, to Richmond, and only about fifteen miles from the latter place, there stands a somewhat ancient and famous public tavern, quite notorious in its better days, as being the grand resort for most of the leading gamblers, horse-racers, cock-fighters, and slave-traders from all the country round about. This old rookery, the nucleus of all sorts of birds, mostly those of ill omen, has, like everything else peculiar to Virginia, lost much of its ancient consequence and splendor; yet it keeps up some appearance of gaiety and high life, and is still frequented, even by respectable travellers, who are unacquainted with its past history and present condition. Its fine old portico looks well at a distance, and gives the building an air of grandeur. A nearer view, however, does little to sustain this pretension. The house is large, and its style imposing, but time and dissipation, unfailing in their results, have made ineffaceable marks upon it, and it must, in the common course of events, soon be numbered with the things that were. The gloomy mantle of ruin is, already, outspread to envelop it, and its remains, even but now remind one of a human skull, after the flesh has mingled with the earth. Old hats and rags fill the places in the upper windows once occupied by large panes of glass, and the moulding boards along the roofing have dropped off from their places, leaving holes and crevices in the rented wall for bats and swallows to build their nests in. The platform of the portico, which fronts the highway is a rickety affair, its planks are loose, and in some places entirely gone, leaving effective man-traps in their stead for nocturnal ramblers. The wooden pillars, which once supported it, but which now hang as encumbrances, are all rotten, and tremble with the touch. A part of the stable, a fine old structure in its day, which has given comfortable shelter to hundreds of the noblest steeds of "the Old Dominion" at once, was blown down many years ago, and never has been, and probably never will be, rebuilt. The doors of the barn are in wretched condition; they will shut with a little human strength to help their worn out hinges, but not otherwise. The side of the great building seen from the road is much discolored in sundry places by slops poured from the upper windows, rendering it unsightly and offensive in other respects. Three or four great dogs, looking as dull and gloomy as the mansion itself, lie stretched out along the door-sills under the portico; and double the number of loafers, some of them completely rum-ripe, and others ripening, dispose themselves like so many sentinels about the front of the house. These latter understand the science of scraping acquaintance to perfection. They know every-body, and almost every-body knows them. Of course, as their title implies, they have no regular employment. They are (to use an expressive phrase) *hangers on*, or still better, they are what sailors would denominate *holders-on to the slack, in every-body's mess, and in nobody's watch*. They are, however, as good as the newspaper for the events of the day, and they sell their knowledge almost as cheap. Money they seldom have; yet they always have capital the most reliable. They make their way with a succeeding traveller by intelligence gained from a preceding one. All the great names of Virginia they know by heart, and have seen their owners often. The history of the house is folded in their lips, and they rattle off stories in connection with it, equal to the guides at Dryburgh Abbey. He must be a shrewd man, and well skilled in the art of evasion, who gets out of the hands of these fellows without being at the expense of a treat.

It was at this old tavern, while on a second visit to the State of Virginia in 1841, that Mr. Listwell, unacquainted with the fame of the place, turned aside, about sunset, to pass the night. Riding up to the house, he had scarcely dismounted, when one of the half dozen bar-room fraternity met and addressed him in a manner exceedingly bland and accommodating.

"Fine evening, sir."

"Very fine," said Mr. Listwell. "This is a tavern, I believe?"

"O yes, sir, yes; although you may think it looks a little the worse for wear, it was once as good a house as any in Virginy. I make no doubt if ye spend the night here, you'll think it a good house yet; for there aint a more accommodating man in the country than you'll find the landlord."

Listwell. "The most I want is a good bed for myself, and a full manger for my horse. If I get these, I shall be quite satisfied."

Loafer. "Well, I alloys like to hear a gentleman talk for his horse; and just becase the horse can't talk for itself. A man that don't care about his beast, and don't look arter it when he's travelling, aint much in my eye anyhow. Now, sir, I likes a horse, and I'll guarantee your horse will be taken good care on here. That old stable, for all you see it looks so shabby now, once sheltered the great *Eclipse*, when he run here agin *Batchelor* and *Jumping Jemmy*. Them was fast horses, but he beat 'em both."

Listwell. "Indeed."

Loafer. "Well, I rather reckon you've travelled a right smart distance to-day, from the look of your horse?"

Listwell. "Forty miles only."

Loafer. "Well! I'll be darned if that aint a pretty good *only*. Mister, that beast of yours is a singed cat, I warrant you. I never see'd a creature like that that wasn't good on the road. You've come about forty miles, then?"

Listwell. "Yes, yes, and a pretty good pace at that."

Loafer. "You're somewhat in a hurry, then, I make no doubt? I reckon I could guess if I would, what you're going to Richmond for? It wouldn't be much of a guess either; for it's rumored hereabouts, that there's to be the greatest sale of niggers at Richmond to-morrow that has taken place there in a long time; and I'll be bound you're a going there to have a hand in it."

Listwell. "Why, you must think, then, that there's money to be made at that business?"

Loafer. "Well, 'pon my honor, sir, I never made any that way myself; but it stands to reason that it's a money making business; for almost all other business in Virginia is dropped to engage in this. One thing is sartain, I never see'd a nigger-buyer yet that hadn't a plenty of money, and he wasn't as free with it as water. I has known one on 'em to treat as high as twenty times in a night; and, generally speaking, they's men of edication, and knows all about the government. The fact is, sir, I alloys like to hear 'em talk, bekase I alloys can learn something from them."

Listwell. "What may I call your name, sir?"

Loafer. "Well, now, they calls me Wilkes. I'm known all around by the gentlemen that comes here. They all knows old Wilkes."

Listwell. "Well, Wilkes, you seem to be acquainted here, and I see you have a strong liking for a horse. Be so good as to speak a kind word for mine to the hostler to-night, and you'll not lose anything by it."

Loafer. "Well, sir, I see you don't say much, but you've got an insight into things. It's alloys wise to get the good will of them that's acquainted about a tavern; for a man don't know when he goes into a house what may happen, or how much he may need a friend." Here the loafer gave Mr. Listwell a significant grin, which expressed a sort of triumphant pleasure at having, as he supposed, by his tact succeeded in placing so fine appearing a gentleman under obligations to him.

THE HEROIC SLAVE. 113

The pleasure, however, was mutual; for there was something so insinuating in the glance of this loquacious customer, that Mr. Listwell was very glad to get quit of him, and to do so more successfully, he ordered his supper to be brought to him in his private room, private to the eye, but not to the ear. This room was directly over the bar, and the plastering being off, nothing but pine boards and naked laths separated him from the disagreeable company below,—he could easily hear what was said in the bar-room, and was rather glad of the advantage it afforded, for, as you shall see, it furnished him important hints as to the manner and deportment he should assume during his stay at that tavern.

Mr. Listwell says he had got into his room but a few moments, when he heard the officious Wilkes below, in a tone of disappointment, exclaim, "Whar's that gentleman?" Wilkes was evidently expecting to meet with his friend at the bar-room, on his return, and had no doubt of his doing the handsome thing. "He has gone to his room," answered the landlord, "and has ordered his supper to be brought to him."

Here some one shouted out, "Who is he, Wilkes? Where's he going?"

"Well, now, I'll be hanged if I know; but I'm willing to make any man a bet of this old hat agin a five dollar bill, that that gent is as full of money as a dog is of fleas. He's going down to Richmond to buy niggers, I make no doubt. He's no fool, I warrant ye."

"Well, he acts d—d strange," said another, "anyhow. I likes to see a man, when he comes up to a tavern, to come straight into the bar-room, and show that he's a man among men. Nobody was going to bite him."

"Now, I don't blame him a bit for not coming in here. That man knows his business, and means to take care on his money," answered Wilkes.

"Wilkes, you're a fool. You only say that, becase you hope to get a few coppers out on him."

"You only measure my corn by your half-bushel, I won't say that you're only mad becase I got the chance of speaking to him first."

"O Wilkes! you're known here. You'll praise up any body that will give you a copper; besides, 'tis my opinion that that fellow who took his long slab-sides up stairs, for all the world just like a half-scared woman, afraid to look honest men in the face, is a *Northerner*, and as mean as dishwater."

"Now what will you bet of that," said Wilkes.

The speaker said, "I make no bets with you, 'kase you can get that fellow up stairs there to say anything."

"Well," said Wilkes, "I am willing to bet any man in the company that *that* gentleman is a *nigger*-buyer. He didn't tell me so right down, but I reckon I knows enough about men to give a pretty clean guess as to what they are arter."

The dispute as to *who* Mr. Listwell was, what his business, where he was going, etc., was kept up with much animation for some time, and more than once threatened a serious disturbance of the peace. Wilkes had his friends as well as his opponents. After this sharp debate, the company amused themselves by drinking whiskey, and telling stories. The latter consisting of quarrels, fights, *rencontres*, and duels, in which distinguished persons of that neighborhood, and frequenters of that house, had been actors. Some of these stories were frightful enough, and were told, too, with a relish which bespoke the pleasure of the parties with the horrid scenes they portrayed. It would not be proper here to give the reader any idea of the vulgarity and dark profanity which rolled, as "a sweet morsel," under these corrupt tongues. A more brutal set of creatures, perhaps, never congregated.

Disgusted, and a little alarmed withal, Mr. Listwell, who was not accustomed to such entertainment, at length retired, but not to sleep. He was *too* much wrought upon by what he had heard to rest quietly, and what snatches of sleep he got, were interrupted by dreams which were anything than pleasant. At eleven o'clock, there seemed to be several hundreds of persons crowding into the house. A loud and confused clamour, cursing and cracking of whips, and the noise of chains startled him from his bed; for a moment he would have given the half of his farm in Ohio to have been at home. This uproar was kept up with undulating course, till near morning. There was loud laughing,—loud singing,—loud cursing,—and yet there seemed to be weeping and mourning in the midst of all. Mr. Listwell said he had heard enough during the forepart of the night to convince him that a buyer of men and women stood the best chance of being respected. And he, therefore, thought it best to say nothing which might undo the favorable opinion that had been formed of him in the bar-room by at least one of the fraternity that swarmed about it. While he would not avow himself a purchaser of slaves, he deemed it not prudent to disavow it. He felt that he might, properly, refuse to cast such a pearl before parties which, to him, were worse than swine. To reveal himself, and to impart a knowledge of his real character and sentiments would, to say the least, be imparting intelligence with the certainty of seeing it and himself both abused. Mr. Listwell confesses, that this reasoning did not altogether satisfy his conscience, for, hating slavery as he did, and regarding it to be the immediate duty of every man to cry out against it, "without compromise and without concealment," it was hard for him to admit to himself the possibility of circumstances wherein a man might, properly, hold his tongue on the subject. Having as little of the spirit of a martyr as Erasmus, he concluded, like the latter, that it was wiser to trust the mercy of God for his soul, than the humanity of slave-traders for his body. Bodily fear, not conscientious scruples, prevailed.

In this spirit he rose early in the morning, manifesting no surprise at what he had heard during the night. His quondam friend was soon at his elbow, boring him with all sorts of questions. All, however, directed to find out his character, business, residence, purposes, and destination. With the most perfect appearance of good nature and carelessness, Mr. Listwell evaded these meddlesome inquiries, and turned conversation to general topics, leaving himself and all that specially pertained to him, out of discussion. Disengaging himself from their troublesome companionship, he made his way towards an old bowling-alley, which was connected with the house, and which, like all the rest, was in very bad repair.

On reaching the alley Mr. Listwell saw, for the first time in his life, a slave-gang

THE HEROIC SLAVE. 115

on their way to market. A sad sight truly. Here were one hundred and thirty human beings,—children of a common Creator—guilty of no crime—men and women, with hearts, minds, and deathless spirits, chained and fettered, and bound for the market, in a christian country,—in a country boasting of its liberty, independence, and high civilization! Humanity converted into merchandise, and linked in iron bands, with no regard to decency or humanity! All sizes, ages, and sexes, mothers, fathers, daughters, brothers, sisters,—all huddled together, on their way to market to be sold and separated from home, and from each other *forever*. And all to fill the pockets of men too lazy to work for an honest living, and who gain their fortune by plundering the helpless, and trafficking in the souls and sinews of men. As he gazed upon this revolting and heart-rending scene, our informant said he almost doubted the existence of a God of justice! And he stood wondering that the earth did not open and swallow up such wickedness.

In the midst of these reflections, and while running his eye up and down the fettered ranks, he met the glance of one whose face he thought he had seen before. To be resolved, he moved towards the spot. It was MADISON WASHINGTON! Here was a scene for the pencil! Had Mr. Listwell been confronted by one risen from the dead, he could not have been more appalled. He was completely stunned. A thunderbolt could not have struck him more dumb. He stood, for a few moments, as motionless as one petrified; collecting himself, he at length exclaimed, "*Madison! is that you?*"

The noble fugitive, but little less astonished than himself, answered cheerily, "O yes, sir, they've got me again."

Thoughtless of consequences for the moment, Mr. Listwell ran up to his old friend, placing his hands upon his shoulders, and looked him in the face! Speechless they stood gazing at each other as if to be doubly resolved that there was no mistake about the matter, till Madison motioned his friend away, intimating a fear lest the keepers should find him there, and suspect him of tampering with the slaves.

"They will soon be out to look after us. You can come when they go to breakfast, and I will tell you all."

Pleased with this arrangement, Mr. Listwell passed out of the alley; but only just in time to save himself, for, while near the door, he observed three men making their way to the alley. The thought occurred to him to await their arrival, as the best means of diverting the ever ready suspicions of the guilty.

While the scene between Mr. Listwell and his friend Madison was going on, the other slaves stood as mute spectators,—at a loss to know what all this could mean. As he left, he heard the man chained to Madison ask, "Who is that gentleman?"

"He is a friend of mine. I cannot tell you now. Suffice it to say he is a friend. You shall hear more of him before long, but mark me! whatever shall pass between that gentleman and me, in your hearing, I pray you will say nothing about it. We are all chained here together,—ours is a common lot; and that gentleman is not less *your* friend than *mine*." At these words, all mysterious as they were, the unhappy company gave signs of satisfaction and hope. It seems that Madison, by that mesmeric power which is the invariable accompaniment of genius, had already won the confidence of the gang, and was a sort of general-in-chief among them.

By this time the keepers arrived. A horrid trio, well fitted for their demoniacal work. Their uncombed hair came down over foreheads *"villainously low,"* and with eyes, mouths, and noses to match. "Hallo! hallo!" they growled out as they entered. "Are you all there!"

"All here," said Madison.

"Well, well, that's right! your journey will soon be over. You'll be in Richmond by eleven to-day, and then you'll have an easy time on it."

"I say, gal, what in the devil are you crying about?" said one of them. "I'll give you something to cry about, if you don't mind." This was said to a girl, apparently not more than twelve years old, who had been weeping bitterly. She had, probably, left behind her a loving mother, affectionate sisters, brothers, and friends, and her tears were but the natural expression of her sorrow, and the only solace. But the dealers in human flesh have *no* respect for such sorrow. They look upon it as a protest against their cruel injustice, and they are prompt to punish it.

This is a puzzle not easily solved. *How* came he here? what can I do for him? may I not even now be in some way compromised in this affair? were thoughts that troubled Mr. Listwell, and made him eager for the promised opportunity of speaking to Madison.

The bell now sounded for breakfast, and keepers and drivers, with pistols and bowie-knives gleaming from their belts, hurried in, as if to get the best places. Taking the chance now afforded, Mr. Listwell hastened back to the bowling-alley. Reaching Madison, he said, "Now *do* tell me all about the matter. Do you know me?"

"Oh, yes," said Madison, "I know you well, and shall never forget you nor that cold and dreary night you gave me shelter. I must be short," he continued, "for they'll soon be out again. This, then, is the story in brief. On reaching Canada, and getting over the excitement of making my escape, sir, my thoughts turned to my poor wife, who had well deserved my love by her virtuous fidelity and undying affection for me. I could not bear the thought of leaving her in the cruel jaws of slavery, without making an effort to rescue her. First, I tried to get money to buy her; but oh! the process was *too slow*. I despaired of accomplishing it. She was in all my thoughts by day, and my dreams by night. At times I could almost hear her voice, saying, 'O Madison! Madison! will you then leave me here? can you leave me here to die? No! no! you will come! you will come!' I was wretched. I lost my appetite. I could neither work, eat, nor sleep, till I resolved to hazard my own liberty, to gain that of my wife! But I must be short. Six weeks ago I reached my old master's place. I laid about the neighborhood nearly a week, watching my chance, and, finally, I ventured upon the desperate attempt to reach my poor wife's room by means of a ladder. I reached the window, but the noise in raising it frightened my wife, and she screamed and fainted. I took her in my arms, and was descending the ladder, when the dogs began to bark furiously, and before I could

THE HEROIC SLAVE. 117

get to the woods the white folks were roused. The cool night air soon restored my wife, and she readily recognized me. We made the best of our way to the woods, but it was now *too* late,—the dogs were after us as though they would have torn us to pieces. It was all over with me now! My old master and his two sons ran out with loaded rifles, and before we were out of gunshot, our ears were assailed with '*Stop! stop! or be shot down.*' Nevertheless we ran on. Seeing that we gave no heed to their calls, they fired, and my poor wife fell by my side dead, while I received but a slight flesh wound. I now became desperate, and stood my ground, and awaited their attack over her dead body. They rushed upon me, with their rifles in hand. I parried their blows, and fought them 'till I was knocked down and overpowered."

"Oh! it was madness to have returned," said Mr. Listwell.

"Sir, I could not be free with the galling thought that my poor wife was still a slave. With her in slavery, my body, not my spirit, was free. I was taken to the house,—chained to a ring-bolt,—my wounds dressed. I was kept there three days. All the slaves, for miles around, were brought to see me. Many slave-holders came with their slaves, using me as proof of the completeness of their power, and of the impossibility of slaves getting away. I was taunted, jeered at, and berated by them, in a manner that pierced me to the soul. Thank God, I was able to smother my rage, and to bear it all with seeming composure. After my wounds were nearly healed, I was taken to a tree and stripped, and I received sixty lashes on my naked back. A few days after, I was sold to a slave-trader, and placed in this gang for the New Orleans market."

"Do you think your master would sell you to me?"

"O no, sir! I was sold on condition of my being taken South. Their motive is revenge."

"Then, then," said Mr. Listwell, "I fear I can do nothing for you. Put your trust in God, and bear your sad lot with the manly fortitude which becomes a man. I shall see you at Richmond, but don't recognize me." Saying this, Mr. Listwell handed Madison ten dollars; said a few words to the other slaves; received their hearty "God bless you," and made his way to the house.

Fearful of exciting suspicion by too long delay, our friend went to the breakfast table, with the air of one who half reproved the greediness of those who rushed in at the sound of the bell. A cup of coffee was all that he could manage. His feelings were too bitter and excited, and his heart was too full with the fate of poor Madison (whom he loved as well as admired) to relish his breakfast; and although he sat long after the company had left the table, he really did little more than change the position of his knife and fork. The strangeness of meeting again one whom he had met on two several occasions before, under extraordinary circumstances, was well calculated to suggest the idea that a supernatural power, a wakeful providence, or an inexorable fate, had linked their destiny together; and that no efforts of his could disentangle him from the mysterious web of circumstances which enfolded him.

On leaving the table, Mr. Listwell nerved himself up and walked firmly into the bar-room. He was at once greeted again by that talkative chatter-box, Mr. Wilkes.

"Them's a likely set of niggers in the alley there," said Wilkes.

"Yes, they're fine looking fellows, one of them I should like to purchase, and for him I would be willing to give a handsome sum."

Turning to one of his comrades, and with a grin of victory, Wilkes said, "Aha, Bill, did you hear that? I told you I know'd that gentleman wanted to buy niggers, and would bid as high as any purchaser in the market."

"Come, come," said Listwell, "don't be too loud in your praise, you are old enough to know that prices rise when purchasers are plenty."

"That's a fact," said Wilkes, "I see you knows the ropes—and there's not a man in old Virginy whom I'd rather help to make a good bargain than you, sir."

Mr. Listwell here threw a dollar at Wilkes, (which the latter caught with a dexterous hand,) saying, "Take that for your kind good will." Wilkes held up the dollar to his right eye, with a grin of victory, and turned to the morose grumbler in the corner who had questioned the liberality of a man of whom he knew nothing.

Mr. Listwell now stood as well with the company as any other occupant of the bar-room.

We pass over the hurry and bustle, the brutal vociferations of the slave-drivers in getting their unhappy gang in motion for Richmond; and we need not narrate every application of the lash to those who faltered in the journey. Mr. Listwell followed the train at a long distance, with a sad heart; and on reaching Richmond, left his horse at a hotel, and made his way to the wharf in the direction of which he saw the slave-coffle driven. He was just in time to see the whole company embark for New Orleans. The thought struck him that, while mixing with the multitude, he might do his friend Madison one last service, and he stept into a hardware store and purchased three strong *files*. These he took with him, and standing near the small boat, which lay in waiting to bear the company by parcels to the side of the brig that lay in the stream, he managed, as Madison passed him, to slip the files into his pocket, and at once darted back among the crowd.

All the company now on board, the imperious voice of the captain sounded, and instantly a dozen hardy seamen were in the rigging, hurrying aloft to unfurl the broad canvas of our Baltimore built American Slaver. The sailors hung about the ropes, like so many black cats, now in the round-tops, now in the cross-trees, now on the yard-arms; all was bluster and activity. Soon the broad fore topsail, the royal and top gallant sail were spread to the breeze. Round went the heavy windlass, clank, clank went the fall-bit,—the anchors weighed,—jibs, mainsails, and topsails hauled to the wind, and the long, low, black slaver, with her cargo of human flesh, careened and moved forward to the sea.

Mr. Listwell stood on the shore, and watched the slaver till the last speck of her upper sails faded from sight, and announced the limit of human vision. "Farewell! farewell! brave and true man! God grant that brighter skies may smile upon your future than have yet looked down upon your thorny pathway."

Saying this to himself, our friend lost no time in completing his business, and in making his way homewards, gladly shaking off from his feet the dust of Old Virginia.

PART IV.

Oh, where's the slave so lowly
Condemn'd to chains unholy,
Who could he burst
His bonds at first
Would pine beneath them slowly?

Moore.

— —Know ye not
Who would be free, *themselves* must strike the blow.

Childe Harold.

What a world of inconsistency, as well as of wickedness, is suggested by the smooth and gliding phrase, AMERICAN SLAVE TRADE; and how strange and perverse is that moral sentiment which loathes, execrates, and brands as piracy and as deserving of death the carrying away into captivity men, women, and children from the *African coast*; but which is neither shocked nor disturbed by a similar traffic, carried on with the same motives and purposes, and characterized by even *more* odious peculiarities on the coast of our MODEL REPUBLIC. We execrate and hang the wretch guilty of this crime on the coast of Guinea, while we respect and applaud the guilty participators in this murderous business on the enlightened shores of the Chesapeake. The inconsistency is so flagrant and glaring, that it would seem to cast a doubt on the doctrine of the innate moral sense of mankind.

Just two months after the sailing of the Virginia slave brig, which the reader has seen move off to sea so proudly with her human cargo for the New Orleans market, there chanced to meet, in the Marine Coffee-house at Richmond, a company of *ocean birds*, when the following conversation, which throws some light on the subsequent history, not only of Madison Washington, but of the hundred and thirty human beings with whom we last saw him chained.

"I say, shipmate, you had rather rough weather on your late passage to Orleans?" said Jack Williams, a regular old salt, tauntingly, to a trim, compact, manly looking person, who proved to be the first mate of the slave brig in question.

"Foul play, as well as foul weather," replied the firmly knit personage, evidently but little inclined to enter upon a subject which terminated so ingloriously to the captain and officers of the American slaver.

"Well, betwixt you and me," said Williams, "that whole affair on board of the Creole was miserably and disgracefully managed. Those black rascals got the upper hand of ye altogether; and, in my opinion, the whole disaster was the result of ignorance of the real character of *darkies* in general. With half a dozen *resolute* white men, (I say it not boastingly,) I could have had the rascals in irons in ten minutes, not because I'm so strong, but I know how to manage 'em. With my back against the *caboose*, I could, myself, have flogged a dozen of them; and had I been on board, by every monster of the deep, every black devil of 'em all would have had his neck stretched from the yard-arm. Ye made a mistake in yer manner of fighting 'em. All that is needed in dealing with a set of rebellious *darkies*, is to show that yer not afraid of 'em. For my own part, I would not honor a dozen niggers by pointing a gun at one on 'em,—a good stout whip, or a stiff rope's end, is better than all the guns at Old Point to quell a *nigger* insurrection. Why, sir, to take a gun to a *nigger* is the best way you can select to tell him you are afraid of him, and the best way of inviting his attack."

This speech made quite a sensation among the company, and a part of them indicated solicitude for the answer which might be made to it. Our first mate replied, "Mr. Williams, all that you've now said sounds very well *here* on shore, where, perhaps, you have studied negro character. I do not profess to understand the subject as well as yourself; but it strikes me, you apply the same rule in dissimilar cases. It is quite easy to talk of flogging niggers here on land, where you have the sympathy of the community, and the whole physical force of the government, State and national, at your command; and where, if a negro shall lift his hand against a white man, the whole community, with one accord, are ready to unite in shooting him down. I say, in such circumstances, it's easy to talk of flogging negroes and of negro cowardice; but, sir, I deny that the negro is, naturally, a coward, or that your theory of managing slaves will stand the test of *salt* water. It may do very well for an overseer, a contemptible hireling, to take advantage of fears already in existence, and which his presence has no power to inspire; to swagger about whip in hand, and discourse on the timidity and cowardice of negroes; for they have a smooth sea and a fair wind. It is one thing to manage a company of slaves on a Virginia plantation, and quite another thing to quell an insurrection on the lonely billows of the Atlantic, where every breeze speaks of courage and liberty. For the negro to act cowardly on shore, may be to act wisely; and I've some doubts whether *you*, Mr. Williams, would find it very convenient were you a slave in Algiers, to raise your hand against the bayonets of a whole government."

"By George, shipmate," said Williams, "you're coming rather *too* near. Either I've fallen very low in your estimation, or your notions of negro courage have got up a button-hole too high. Now I more than ever wish I'd been on board of that luckless craft. I'd have given ye practical evidence of the truth of my theory. I don't doubt there's some difference in being at sea. But a nigger's a nigger, on sea or land; and is a coward, find him where you will; a drop of blood from one on 'em will skeer a hundred. A knock on the nose, or a kick on the shin, will tame the wildest '*darkey*' you can fetch me. I say again, and will stand by it, I could, with half a dozen good men, put the whole nineteen on 'em in irons, and have carried them safe to New Orleans too. Mind, I don't blame you, but I do say, and every gentleman here will bear me out in it, that the fault was somewhere, or them niggers would never have got off as they have done. For my part I feel ashamed to have the idea go abroad, that a ship load of slaves can't be safely taken from Richmond to New Orleans. I should like, merely to redeem the character of Virginia sailors, to take charge of a ship load on 'em to-morrow."

THE HEROIC SLAVE.

Williams went on in this strain, occasionally casting an imploring glance at the company for applause for his wit, and sympathy for his contempt of negro courage. He had, evidently, however, waked up the wrong passenger; for besides being in the right, his opponent carried that in his eye which marked him a man not to be trifled with.

"Well, sir," said the sturdy mate, "you can select your own method for distinguishing yourself;—the path of ambition in this direction is quite open to you in Virginia, and I've no doubt that you will be highly appreciated and compensated for all your valiant achievements in that line; but for myself, while I do not profess to be a giant, I have resolved never to set my foot on the deck of a slave ship, either as officer, or common sailor again; I have got enough of it."

"Indeed! indeed!" exclaimed Williams, derisively.

"Yes, *indeed*," echoed the mate; "but don't misunderstand me. It is not the high value that I set upon my life that makes me say what I have said; yet I'm resolved never to endanger my life again in a cause which my conscience does not approve. I dare say *here* what many men *feel*, but *dare not speak*, that this whole slave-trading business is a disgrace and scandal to Old Virginia."

"Hold! hold on! shipmate," said Williams, "I hardly thought you'd have shown your colors so soon,—I'll be hanged if you're not as good an abolitionist as Garrison himself."

The mate now rose from his chair, manifesting some excitement. "What do you mean, sir," said he, in a commanding tone. "*That man does not live who shall offer me an insult with impunity.*"

The effect of these words was marked; and the company clustered around. Williams, in an apologetic tone, said, "Shipmate! keep your temper. I mean't no insult. We all know that Tom Grant is no coward, and what I said about your being an abolitionist was simply this: you *might* have put down them black mutineers and murderers, but your conscience held you back."

"In that, too," said Grant, "you were mistaken. I did all that any man with equal strength and presence of mind could have done. The fact is, Mr. Williams, you underrate the courage as well as the skill of these negroes, and further, you do not seem to have been correctly informed about the case in hand at all."

"All I know about it is," said Williams, "that on the ninth day after you left Richmond, a dozen or two of the niggers ye had on board, came on deck and took the ship from you;—had her steered into a British port, where, by the by, every woolly head of them went ashore and was free. Now I take this to be a discreditable piece of business, and one demanding explanation."

"There are a great many discreditable things in the world," said Grant. "For a ship to go down under a calm sky is, upon the first flush of it, disgraceful either to sailors or caulkers. But when we learn, that by some mysterious disturbance in nature, the waters parted beneath, and swallowed the ship up, we lose our indignation and disgust in lamentation of the disaster, and in awe of the Power which controls the elements."

"Very true, very true," said Williams, "I should be very glad to have an explanation which would relieve the affair of its present discreditable features. I have desired to see you ever since you got home, and to learn from you a full statement of the facts in the case. To me the whole thing seems unaccountable. I cannot see how a dozen or two of ignorant negroes, not one of whom had ever been to sea before, and all of them were closely ironed between decks, should be able to get their fetters off, rush out of the hatchway in open daylight, kill two white men, the one the captain and the other their master, and then carry the ship into a British port, where every '*darkey*' of them was set free. There must have been great carelessness, or cowardice somewhere!"

The company which had listened in silence during most of this discussion, now became much excited. One said, I agree with Williams; and several said the thing looks black enough. After the temporary tumultous exclamations had subsided,—

"I see," said Grant, "how you regard this case, and how difficult it will be for me to render our ship's company blameless in your eyes. Nevertheless, I will state the fact precisely as they came under my own observation. Mr. Williams speaks of 'ignorant negroes,' and, as a general rule, they are ignorant; but had he been on board the *Creole* as I was, he would have seen cause to admit that there are exceptions to this general rule. The leader of the mutiny in question was just as shrewd a fellow as ever I met in my life, and was as well fitted to lead in a dangerous enterprise as any one white man in ten thousand. The name of this man, strange to say, (ominous of greatness,) was MADISON WASHINGTON. In the short time he had been on board, he had secured the confidence of every officer. The negroes fairly worshipped him. His manner and bearing were such, that no one could suspect him of a murderous purpose. The only feeling with which we regarded him was, that he was a powerful, good-disposed negro. He seldom spake to any one, and when he did speak, it was with the utmost propriety. His words were well chosen, and his pronunciation equal to that of any schoolmaster. It was a mystery to us *where* he got his knowledge of language; but as little was said to him, none of us knew the extent of his intelligence and ability till it was too late. It seems he brought three files with him on board, and must have gone to work upon his fetters the first night out; and he must have worked well at that; for on the day of the rising, he got the irons *off eighteen* besides himself.

"The attack began just about twilight in the evening. Apprehending a squall, I had commanded the second mate to order all hands on deck, to take in sail. A few minutes before this I had seen Madison's head above the hatchway, looking out upon the white-capped waves at the leeward. I think I never saw him look more good-natured. I stood just about midship, on the larboard side. The captain was pacing the quarter-deck on the starboard side, in company with Mr. Jameson, the owner of most of the slaves on board. Both were armed. I had just told the men to lay aloft, and was looking to see my orders obeyed, when I heard the discharge of a pistol on the starboard side; and turning suddenly around, the very deck seemed covered with fiends from the pit. The nineteen negroes were all on deck, with their broken fetters in their hands, rushing in all directions. I put my hand quickly in my

THE HEROIC SLAVE. 123

pocket to draw out my jack-knife; but before I could draw it, I was knocked senseless to the deck. When I came to myself, (which I did in a few minutes, I suppose, for it was yet quite light,) there was not a white man on deck. The sailors were all aloft in the rigging, and dared not come down. Captain Clarke and Mr. Jameson lay stretched on the quarter-deck,—both dying,—while Madison himself stood at the helm unhurt.

"I was completely weakened by the loss of blood, and had not recovered from the stunning blow which felled me to the deck; but it was a little too much for me, even in my prostrate condition, to see our good brig commanded by a *black murderer*. So I called out to the men to come down and take the ship, or die in the attempt. Suiting the action to the word, I started aft. You murderous villain, said I, to the imp at the helm, and rushed upon him to deal him a blow, when he pushed me back with his strong, black arm, as though I had been a boy of twelve. I looked around for the men. They were still in the rigging. Not one had come down. I started towards Madison again. The rascal now told me to stand back. 'Sir,' said he, 'your life is in my hands. I could have killed you a dozen times over during this last half hour, and could kill you now. You call me a *black murderer*. I am not a murderer. God is my witness that LIBERTY, not *malice*, is the motive for this night's work. I have done no more to those dead men yonder, than they would have done to me in like circumstances. We have struck for our freedom, and if a true man's heart be in you, you will honor us for the deed. We have done that which you applaud your fathers for doing, and if we are murderers, *so were they*.'

"I felt little disposition to reply to this impudent speech. By heaven, it disarmed me. The fellow loomed up before me. I forgot his blackness in the dignity of his manner, and the eloquence of his speech. It seemed as if the souls of both the great dead (whose names he bore) had entered him. To the sailors in the rigging he said: 'Men! the battle is over,—your captain is dead. I have complete command of this vessel. All resistance to my authority will be in vain. My men have won their liberty, with no other weapons but their own BROKEN FETTERS. We are nineteen in number. We do not thirst for your blood, we demand only our rightful freedom. Do not flatter yourselves that I am ignorant of chart or compass. I know both. We are now only about sixty miles from Nassau. Come down, and do your duty. Land us in Nassau, and not a hair of your heads shall be hurt.'

"I shouted, *Stay where you are, men*,—when a sturdy black fellow ran at me with a handspike, and would have split my head open, but for the interference of Madison, who darted between me and the blow. 'I know what you are up to,' said the latter to me. 'You want to navigate this brig into a slave port, where you would have us all hanged; but you'll miss it; before this brig shall touch a slave-cursed shore while I am on board, I will myself put a match to the magazine, and blow her, and be blown with her, into a thousand fragments. Now I have saved your life twice within these last twenty minutes,—for, when you lay helpless on deck, my men were about to kill you. I held them in check. And if you now (seeing I am your friend and not your enemy) persist in your resistance to my authority, I give you fair warning, YOU SHALL DIE.'

"Saying this to me, he cast a glance into the rigging where the terror-stricken sailors were clinging, like so many frightened monkeys, and commanded them to come down, in a tone from which there was no appeal; for four men stood by with muskets in hand, ready at the word of command to shoot them down.

"I now became satisfied that resistance was out of the question; that my best policy was to put the brig into Nassau, and secure the assistance of the American consul at that port. I felt sure that the authorities would enable us to secure the murderers, and bring them to trial.

"By this time the apprehended squall had burst upon us. The wind howled furiously,—the ocean was white with foam, which, on account of the darkness, we could see only by the quick flashes of lightning that darted occasionally from the angry sky. All was alarm and confusion. Hideous cries came up from the slave women. Above the roaring billows a succession of heavy thunder rolled along, swelling the terrific din. Owing to the great darkness, and a sudden shift of the wind, we found ourselves in the trough of the sea. When shipping a heavy sea over the starboard bow, the bodies of the captain and Mr. Jameson were washed overboard. For awhile we had dearer interests to look after than slave property. A more savage thunder-gust never swept the ocean. Our brig rolled and creaked as if every bolt would be started, and every thread of oakum would be pressed out of the seams. To the pumps! to the pumps! I cried, but not a sailor would quit his grasp. Fortunately this squall soon passed over, or we must have been food for sharks.

"During all the storm, Madison stood firmly at the helm,—his keen eye fixed upon the binnacle. He was not indifferent to the dreadful hurricane; yet he met it with the equanimity of an old sailor. He was silent but not agitated. The first words he uttered after the storm had slightly subsided, were characteristic of the man. 'Mr. mate, you cannot write the bloody laws of slavery on those restless billows. The ocean, if not the land, is free.' I confess, gentlemen, I felt myself in the presence of a superior man; one who, had he been a white man, I would have followed willingly and gladly in any honorable enterprise. Our difference of color was the only ground for difference of action. It was not that his principles were wrong in the abstract; for they are the principles of 1776. But I could not bring myself to recognize their application to one whom I deemed my inferior.

"But to my story. What happened now is soon told. Two hours after the frightful tempest had spent itself, we were plump at the wharf in Nassau. I sent two of our men immediately to our consul with a statement of facts, requesting his interference in our behalf. What he did, or whither he did anything, I don't know; but, by order of the authorities, a company of *black* soldiers came on board, for the purpose, as they said, of protecting the property. These impudent rascals, when I called on them to assist me in keeping the slaves on board, sheltered themselves adroitly under their instructions only to protect property,—and said they did not recognize *persons* as *property*. I told them that by the laws of Virginia and the laws of the United States, the slaves on board were as much property as the barrels of flour in the hold. At this the stupid blockheads showed their *ivory*, rolled up their white eyes in horror, as if the idea of putting men on a footing with merchandise were revolting to their humanity. When these instructions were understood among the negroes, it was impossible for us to keep them on board. They deliberately gathered up their baggage before our eyes, and, against our remonstrances, poured through the gangway,—formed themselves into a procession on the wharf,—bid farewell to all on board, and, uttering the wildest shouts of exultation, they marched, amidst the deafening cheers of a multitude of sympathizing spectators, under the triumphant leadership of their heroic chief and deliverer, MADISON WASHINGTON."

Frederick Douglass.

A PLEA FOR FREE SPEECH.

Give me leave to speak my mind.

As You Like It.

The clamorous demand which certain patriotic gentlemen are just now making for perfect silence on the slavery question, strikes a quiet looker-on as something very odd. It might pass for a dull sort of joke, were it not that the means taken to enforce it, by vexatious prosecutions, political and social proscriptions, and newspaper assaults on private reputation, are beginning, in certain quarters, to assume a decidedly tragic aspect, and forcing upon all anti-slavery men the alternative of peremptorily refusing compliance, or standing meanly by to see others crushed for advocating *their* opinions.

The question has been extensively, and I think very naturally raised, why these anti-agitation gentlemen do not keep silent themselves. For, strange as it may seem, this perilous topic is the very one which most of all appears to occupy their thoughts too, and is ever uppermost when they undertake to speak of the affairs of the country. They are in the predicament of the poor man in the Eastern fable, who, being forbidden on pain of the genie's wrath to utter a certain cabalistic syllable, found, to his horror, that he could never after open his lips without their beginning perversely to frame the tabooed articulation. But not, as in his case, does fear chain up their organs. They speak it boldly out, proclaim it "the corner-stone" of their political creed, and do their best in every way, by speeches and articles, Union-safety pamphlets and National Convention platforms, to "keep it before the people." And the object always is, to keep the people quiet! Surely, if the Union is *not* strong enough to bear agitations, the special friends of the Union have chosen a singular way to save it.

I would by no means infer, that they are *altogether* insecure in their professions of anxiety. The truth appears to be, however, that in so far as these professions are not a sheer pretence, got up by political men for political effect, our estimable fellow citizens have, all unwittingly, been obeying a higher law than that which they would impose on their neighbors,—a law, written in the very nature of the free soul. On this, the subject of the age, they must think, and cannot refrain from uttering their thoughts. "They believe, and *therefore* have they spoken." And it is a sufficient reply to their unanswerable demand for silence on the other side. "We *also* believe, and therefore speak." Pray, why not?

A certain ardent conservative friend of mine, to whom I once proposed this inquiry, made a short answer to it after this fashion:—"The abolitionists are all fools and fanatics. Whenever the idea of anti-slavery gets hold of a man, he takes leave

A PLEA FOR FREE SPEECH.   127

of his common sense, and is thenceforth as one possessed. I would put a padlock on every such crazy fellow's mouth." My friend's rule, it will be seen, is a very broad one; stopping the mouths of all who speak foolishly. Who will undertake to see it fairly applied? or who could feel quite free from nervousness in view of its possible operation? Under an infallible administration, I apprehend, many—some, perhaps, even of the most strenuous advocates of the law—might find themselves uncomfortably implicated, who at present hardly suspect the danger. "By'rlakin, a parlous fear! my masters, you ought to consider with yourselves!" I am constrained to confess, that in the very midst of my friend's aforesaid patriotic diatribe against folly and fanaticism, and his plea for a summary fool-act, I could not keep out of my mind some wicked recollections of Horace's lines:

> *Communi sensu plane caret*, inquimus. Eheu!
> Quam temere in *nosmet* legem sancimus iniquam!

It must in all candor be confessed, that there is something in the subject of slavery which, when fairly looked at and realized, is a little trying to one's sanity. Even such intellects as John Wesley's and Thomas Jefferson's, seem to stagger a little under a view of the appalling sum of iniquity and wretchedness which the word represents, and vent their excitement in terms not particularly measured. What wonder, then, if men of simpler minds should now and then be thrown quite off the balance, and think and say some things that are really unwise. I think, indeed, it will have to be confessed, that we have had fools and fanatics on both sides of the slavery question; and it is altogether among the probabilities, that such will continue to be the case hereafter. Still, until we have some infallible criterion to distinguish actual folly from that which foolish people merely think such, I fancy we must forego the convenience of my friend's summary process, and, giving leave to every man to speak his mind, leave it to Time—great sifter of men and opinions—to separate between the precious and the vile.

It may be the kindness bred of a fellow feeling, but I must confess to a warm side towards my brethren of the motley tribe. While on the one hand I firmly hold with Elihu—who seems to have represented young Uz among the friends of Job—that "great men are not always wise." I rejoice on the other hand in the concession of Polonius,—chief old Fogy of the court of Denmark,—that there is "a happiness which madness often hits on, that reason and sanity could not so prosperously be delivered of." Folly and craziness, quotha! Did it, then, never occur to you, O Worldly Wiseman, that even your wisdom might be bettered by a dash of that which you thus contemptuously brand? Or does the apostle seem to you as one that driveleth, when he says, "If any man among you seemeth to be wise in this world, let him become a fool, that he may be wise?"

I have often admired the sagacity of our mediaeval forefathers, in the treatment of their (so called) fools. They gave them a *special license* of the tongue; for they justly estimated the advantages which the truly wise know how to draw from the untrammelled utterances of any honest mind, especially of minds which, refusing to run tamely in the oiled grooves of prescriptive and fashionable orthodoxy, are the more likely, now and then, (were it only by accident,) to hit upon truths of which others miss. Hence they maintained an "Independent Order" of the motley, whose only business it was freely to think and freely speak their minds. "I must have liberty withal," says Jaques, aspiring to this dignity.

>—"as free a charter as the wind,
>To blow on whom I please: for *so fools have*."

And he adds, in a strain of admonition which certain contemporaneous events might almost lead one to consider prophetic,

>— —"they that are most galled with my folly,
>They most must laugh. And why, sir, must they so?
>The *why* is plain as way to parish church.
>He that a fool doth very wisely hit,
>Doth very foolishly, although he smart,
>Not to seem senseless of the bob. If not,
>The wise man's folly is anatomised
>Even by the squandering glances of the fool.
>* * What then? Let me see wherein
>My speech hath wronged him. If it do him right,
>Then he hath wronged himself; if he be free,
>Why then, my taxing like a wild goose flies,
>Unclaimed of any man."

Now if there be "fools of the nineteenth century," as I devoutly hope there be,—men possessed with the belief of a Higher Law, Inalienable Rights, Supremacy of Conscience, and such like obsolete phantoms, and passing strange judgments on the deeds of men and nations in the light thereof,—I beg to put in a similar plea for them. *Give them leave to speak their minds.* Now and then, it may be worth the pondering, and, heeded betimes, may peradventure save from calamity and ruin. If not, an attempt to *enforce* silence on fools—and is it not much the same with freemen?—is likely to produce, not silence at all, but a greater outcry. And as for our great men and wise men, when hit, let them conceal the smart, and profit by the lesson. But, for their own greatness' sake, and the honor of their wisdom, whither hit or not, let them never fall into a passion at the freedom of men's speech, and cry, *This must be put down.* For it will not down at their bidding.

But the subject refuses to be treated lightly. The vast interests at stake on both sides, and the immediate urgency of the crisis, compel the mind to sobriety and solicitude in the contemplation of it. No truly wise man will look upon the anti-slavery doctrine as mere folly, or on the promulgation of it as idle breath. It is the measureless power of that sentiment—and all its power lies in its truth—that wakens this alarm; and it is the consciousness of holding such a weapon in their hands, that makes the anti-slavery masses at the North pause, lest in attempting to use it for good, they should, unwittingly, do harm. For such a sentiment, who can fail to feel respect? Who would not despise himself if his own bosom were destitute of it? But, by as much as I respect it in others, and would cherish it in myself, by so much will I resent all playing upon it by political men for party or personal ends, and fear lest it betray me into pusillanimity and inertness where the times demand action for humanity and God. It *is* a serious question for all honest anti-slavery men throughout the land, in what way they can most wisely and hopefully quit them of their responsibility in relation to this thing. Their action as citizens should, unquestionably, be restricted by the just limits of their civil responsibility; as men by those of their moral responsibility. Even within those limits, they should act with a wise moderation, and in a generous spirit of candor and kindness. But one thing is abundantly certain, that by ignoring the responsibility, they do not get rid of it; by turning their backs on the obligation, they will not get it discharged. Still the terrible *fact* remains. *Still, the tears and blood of the enslaved are daily dropping on our country's soil.* Throw over it what veil of extenuation and excuse you may, the essential crime and shame remains. Believe as kindly as you can of the treatment which the slaves receive of humane and christian masters; it is only on condition that they first surrender their every *right* as men. Let them dare demur to that, and their tears and blood must answer it. That is the terrible fact; and *our country* is the abettor, the protector, and the agent of the iniquity. Must we be indifferent? *May* we be indifferent? It is a question of tremendous import to every freeman in the land, who honestly believes that the rights he claims as a man are common to the race.

We used to be told, and are sometimes still, that this is a matter which belongs to our Southern brethren exclusively, and that when we of the free States interfere with it, we meddle with that which is "none of our business." And there was a time, when this might be urged with a show of consistency. It was when slavery claimed only to be a creature of State legislation, and asked only of the national government and the free States to be let alone. Even then, it had no right of exemption from the rational scrutiny to which all human institutions are amenable, nor from the rebuke and denouncement which all men may, in Heaven's name, utter against all iniquity done in the face of Heaven. But the *special* right of republican citizens to demand the correction of wrongs done by *their own* government, attached in the matter of slavery only to the citizens of the slave States.

But a wonderful change has been passing before our eyes. The attitude of slavery is entirely altered. It now claims to be nationalized. It demands a distinct recognition and active protection from the general government, and indirect, but most effectual support from every State in the Union, and from every citizen thereof! The government has acknowledged the validity of the claim; and our great political leaders—some on whom we have been wont to rely as stalwart champions of freedom—have turned short round in their tracks, and require us to believe that we are *under constitutional obligations* to help maintain the accursed thing,—yea, through all future time, to do its most menial work! Nor is the doctrine to be left in the dubious region of speculation. It is already "a fixed fact," terribly embodied in a penal law. It enters the home of every Northern freeman, and announces in thunder-tones this ancestral obligation, which had so strangely faded from the recollections of men. It tolerates no dulness of apprehension, no hesitancy of belief. It bids us all, on pain of imprisonments and fines, to conquer our prejudices, to swallow our scruples, to be still with our nonsensical humanities, and, "as good citizens," to start out at the whistle of a United States' constable, to chase down miserable negroes fleeing from the hell of bondage!

Slavery, then, has become *our* business at last; and, as such, does it not behoove us to attend to it? I think, in the language of honest Dogberry, that "that is proved already, and will go near to be thought so shortly." The thing lies in a nutshell. Millard Fillmore is not our master, but our servant. It is not his to prescribe duties, but ours; and his, to perform them. What he does, in his own person and by his subordinate executive officers, he does for us, and on our responsibility. What he does or they do, in other words, we do; and we must abide the reckoning. In this responsibility, the humblest citizen bears his share, and cannot shirk it if he would. When, then, I see the ministers of my country's law consigning men with flesh and blood like my own, with homes and business, with wives and children,

> As dear to them, as are the ruddy drops
> That visit their sad hearts,

men unaccused of crime, and eating the daily bread of honest labor—consigning them, I say, and their posterity to hopeless vassalage, and degrading chattelhood, by a process, too, which tramples under foot the most ancient and sacred guarantees of my own and my neighbors' rights. When I see this great nation lay its terrible grasp upon the throat of a feeble, unoffending man, and thrust him back to worse than a felon's fate for doing that which no casuistry can torture into a crime, I am compelled to feel that *it is myself* engaged in this atrocious business; and no one but myself can rid me of the responsibility. I can no longer be silent; I dare no longer be silent; I will no longer be silent. I will remonstrate and cry, shame! I will refuse to obey the law; I will demand to be released, and to have my country released, from its odious requirements. I will vote, and influence voters, and use every prerogative of freedom, to throw at least from off my conscience a burden that it cannot bear. And who that is worthy to be free himself, will blame me? To speak is no longer a mere right; it has become a religious duty.

Let no man tell me, that this law is a mere dead letter. The old Fugitive Law had, indeed, become so; and so would any other be likely to become, which, while grasping after the slave, should pay a decent respect to the rights of the free. But slavery cannot subsist on any such condition; and this law was framed to supply the deficiencies of the old law, and *to accomplish the thing*. It is based on the assumption that the government of the United States is bound to effect the rendition of fugitives, if possible at all, *at whatever cost*. And, if this law is insufficient, the assumption is equally good for still more stringent measures. But I repeat it, let no man tell me it is *now* a nullity. Have we not seen it executed in our streets, and at our very doors? I chanced to be in the city of New York at the time when, I think, its first victim, Henry Long, was torn from his family, and from a reputable and profitable business, and sent back,—limbs, and brain, and throbbing, loving heart,—the husband, father, friend, the peaceful and industrious member of society,—all, to be the *property* of a fellow-mortal in a hostile land. Could I look upon this crimeless man, thus in the grasp of the officers of my country's laws, my own representatives, and hurried unresisting to that dreadful doom; and ever be able to believe the law innocuous, and myself guiltless while I acquiesced in silence? The rabble followed him along the streets, shouting in exultation at the negro's fate. *Them* I must acknowledge as my fellows and brethren, but *him*—on him I must

A PLEA FOR FREE SPEECH.

put my heel, with theirs, to crush him out of manhood! And the morrow's papers, edited by professed Christians, heralded the occurrence, with not even a decent pretence of pity and regret, but as a triumph of LAW, (O sacred name profaned!) in which all good men should rejoice. That day I felt a stiffing sensation settling down upon me, of which my previous experience had afforded no precedent, and with an oppressive weight which no language can describe. *I felt that I no longer breathed the air of liberty*; that slavery was spreading her Upas branches athwart *my* sky also. The convenient apology that the sin was not mine, but another's, no longer stood me in stead; and I have wondered ever since to hear any honest Northern man employ it. There are Northern men, from whom nothing could surprise me.

And what have we since witnessed? The inferior officers of the law prowling throughout the North for victims on whom to enforce it. Their superiors, even to the highest, laboring by speeches and proclamations and journeyings to and fro in the land (is it too much to say?) to *dragoon* the people into its support. The national treasury thrown wide open to meet its "extraordinary expenses." Fanueil Hall hung in chains, to ensure its execution. Presidential candidates vieing with each other in expressions of attachment and fidelity to it. Able men, in church and State, spotted for proscription for no other sin than hating that law, and daring to declare that hatred. And to crown the whole, the wisdom of the nation, in Baltimore Conventions once and again assembled, pronouncing the new doctrines of constitutional responsibility, with the law that embodies it, not only a certainty, but (hear it, O heavens!) a *finality*! A new word in the political vocabulary, and verily a new thing in the earth! "Finality," in the legislation of freemen! A finality, that forever precludes reconsideration, amendment, or repeal! When such things are said, and gravely said, by men professing to be American statesmen, I can almost imagine the fathers of my country turning painfully in their graves. And can it be possible, that in the same breath with which men assume to roll political responsibilities on freemen, they dare require perpetual silence and unconsidering submission thereto? Then, what is it to be free?

But let no one dream that these formidable pronouncements have any enduring force. It is natural, that Southern statesmen should seek, by every possible expedient, to keep out the flood of discussion from a system which can so illy bear it. And it is not strange, that Northern politicians should, for temporary purposes, assist them in the effort. This is for a day; but the great tide of human thought flows on forever, and there is no spot from which it will be shut out. I remember when the right of petition was denied by our Southern brethren, in respect to this subject; and they found compliant tools enough from the North to work with for a season. But was the right of petition sacrificed? Of course not. And is the right of free discussion, the right to make and (if we please) unmake our laws, less precious? This subject *will* be agitated. This law will be reconsidered; and, if it is not repealed, it will be for the same reasons that ensures the continuance of other laws, namely, because it is able to sustain severe and ever recurring scrutiny.

But what is to become of the Union meanwhile? One thing is very certain. If it deliberately place itself in competition with those "blessings of liberty," which it was created to "secure," it *ought* to fall. Shall the end be sacrificed to preserve the means, to which the end alone gives value? And what are we to think of the statesmanship of those, who, to effect that preservation, would force such an issue on a people nursed at the breasts of freedom? I would rather die than live a traitor to my country; but let me die *ten thousand* deaths before I prove treacherous to freedom and to God. "If this be treason, make the most of it."

But it is worse than idle to talk so. There is no such issue before the nation. We are not compelled to choose between disunion and slavery; a slavery, too, that would not only hold the black man in its remorseless gripe, but put its fetters on the conscience of the white man, and its gag into his mouth. Our Southern brethren themselves, even to save their cherished institution, would not dare, would not desire to press such an alternative. Were it so, who would not be ready to surrender the Union as valueless to him, and to part company with Southrons as men unworthy to be free? But it is not so. There are Hotspurs, doubtless, enough of them at the South; and Jehus, too many, at the North. And there are cunning politicians to stand between the two sections, and play upon the prejudices of both, and into each other's hands, for selfish ends. But the great heart of the nation, North and South, on the whole and according to the measure of its understanding, beats true alike to freedom and the constitution, — true to that immortal sentiment which, as long as this nation endures, shall encircle its author's name with a halo, in whose splendor some later words that have fallen from his lips will be happily lost and forgotten: "Liberty *and* Union, now and forever, one and inseparable." Whatever differences there may be as to the nature, conditions, and obligations of freedom, or as to the intent and meaning of the constitution, no party among the people will refuse to submit them to the ordeal of discussion, and the arbitrament of the appointed tribunals.

While this is so, let him be deemed the traitor, who stands up before the world, and belies his country by declaring it to be otherwise. And let every man prepare to enter into those discussions which no human power can now stave off, in a spirit of intelligent candor and kindness, but, at the same time, of inflexible fidelity to God and man.

Prof. J. H. Raymond

PLACIDO.

The true wealth and glory of a nation consist not in its gold dust, nor in its commerce, nor in the grandeur of its palaces, nor yet in the magnificence of its cities,—but in the intellectual and moral energy of its people. Egypt is more glorious because of her carrying into Greece the blessings of civilization, than because of her pyramids, however wondrous, her lakes and labyrinths, however stupendous, or her Thebes, though every square marked a palace, or every alley a dome. Who hears of the moneyed men of Athens, of Rome? And who does *not* hear of Socrates, of Plato, of Demosthenes, of Virgil, of Cicero? Are you in converse with him of the "Sea-girt Isle," and would touch the chord that vibrates most readily in his heart?—then talk to him of Shakspeare, of Milton, of Cowper, of Bacon, of Newton; of Burns, of Scott. To the intelligent son of the "Emerald Isle," talk of Curran, of Emmett, of O'Connell.

Great men are a nation's vitality. Nations pass away,—great men, never. Great men are not unfrequently buried in dungeons or in obscurity; but they work out great thoughts for all time, nevertheless. Did not Bunyan work out a great thought all-vital and vitalizing, when he lay twelve years in Bedford jail, weaving his tagged lace, and writing his Pilgrim's Progress? The greatest man in all America is now in obscurity. It is he who is *"the Lord of his own soul,"* on whose brow wisdom has marked her supremacy, and who, in his sphere, moves

"Stilly as a star, on his eternal way."

A great writer hath said, "Nature is stingy of her great men." I do not believe it. God doeth all his work fitly and well; how, therefore, could he give us great men, not plentifully, but stingily? The truth is, there are great men, and they are plentiful,—plentiful for the times, I mean,—but we do not see them, because we will not come into the sun-light of truth and rectitude where, and where only, dwelleth greatness.

Placido was a great man. He was a great poet besides. He was a patriot, also,—how could he be otherwise? Are not all poets patriots?

"Adios Mundo," cried he, as with tear-bedimmed eyes he looked up into the blue heavens above him, and upon the green earth beneath him; and upon the portals of the universe read wisdom, majesty, and power. Was there no poetry in this outburst of a full heart, and in this looking upward to heaven? "Adios Mundo," cried he, as now beholding, for the last time, the home of his love,—he bared his bosom to the death-shot of the soldiers.

Great was Placido in life,—he was greater still in death. His was the faith which fastens itself upon the EVERLASTING I AM.

Call you that greatness which Pizarro achieved when, seizing a sword and drawing a line upon the sand from east to west, he himself facing south, he said to his band of pirates:—"*Friends, comrades, on that side are toil, hunger, nakedness, the drenching storm, desertion, and death; on this side, ease and pleasure. There lies Peru with its richness; here Panama with its poverty. Choose, each man what best becomes a brave Castillian. For my part I go to the south;*"—suiting the action to the word? So do I,—but look ye, this is merely the greatness of overwhelming energy and concentrated purpose, not illuminated by a single ray of light from the Divine. See here, how Placido dwarfeth Pizarro when he thus prayeth,

> "God of unbounded love, and power eternal!
> To Thee I turn in darkness and despair;
> Stretch forth Thine arm, and from the brow infernal
> Of calumny the veil of justice tear!
>
> O, King of kings!—my father's God!—who only
> Art strong to save, by whom is all controlled,—
> Who giv'st the sea its waves, the dark and lonely
> Abyss of heaven its light, the North its cold,
> The air its currents, the warm sun its beams,
> Life to the flowers, and motion to the streams:
>
> All things obey Thee; dying or reviving
> As thou commandest; all, apart from Thee,
> From Thee alone their life and power deriving,
> Sink and are lost in vast eternity!
>
> O, merciful God! I cannot shun Thy presence,
> For through its veil of flesh, Thy piercing eye
> Looketh upon my spirit's unsoiled essence,
> As through the pure transparence of the sky;
> Let not the oppressor clap his bloody hands,
> As o'er my prostrate innocence he stands.
>
> But if, alas, it seemeth good to Thee
> That I should perish as the guilty dies,
> Still, fully in me, Thy will be done, O God!"

Placido had a symmetrically developed character. All great men have this. His intellectual and moral nature blended harmoniously as

> "Kindred elements into one."

An ancient philosopher hath said that the passions and the soul are placed in the same body, so that the passions might have ready opportunity to persuade the soul to become subservient to their purpose. A terrible conflict. And yet through it Placido passed triumphantly.

Placido was born a slave on the island of Cuba, on the plantation of Don Terribio De Castro. The year of his birth I am unable to give, but it must have been somewhere between the years 1790 and 1800. He was of African origin. But little

PLACIDO.

is known of his earliest days save that he was of gentle demeanor, and wore an aspect which, though mild, indicated the working of great thoughts within. He was allowed some little advantage of education in his youth, and he evinced great poetic genius. The prayer just quoted was composed by him while he lay in prison, and repeated on his way from his dungeon to his place of execution.

The Heraldo, a leading journal of Havana, thus spoke of him after his arrest:—

"Placido is a celebrated poet,—a man of great genius, but too wild and ambitious. His object was to subdue Cuba, and make himself the chief."

The following lines, also, were found inscribed upon the walls of his dungeon. They were written on the day previous to his execution.

> "O Liberty! I wait for thee,
> To break this chain, and dungeon bar;
> I hear thy voice calling me,
> Deep in the frozen North, afar,
> With voice like God's, and vision like a star.
>
> Long cradled in the mountain wind,
> Thy mates, the eagle and the storm:
> Arise; and from thy brow unbind
> The wreath that gives its starry form,
> And smite the strength, that would thy strength deform.
>
> Yet Liberty! thy dawning light,
> Obscured by dungeon bars, shall cast
> A splendor on the breaking night,
> And tyrants, flying thick and fast,
> Shall tremble at thy gaze, and stand aghast."

In poetic feeling, patriotic spirit, living faith, and, withal in literary beauty, these lines are not surpassed; and they cannot fail to rank Placido not only with the great-hearted, but with the gifted men of the earth. A tribute to his genius is recorded in the fact, that he was ransomed from slavery by the contributions of slave-holders of Cuba.

Placido was executed on the 7th of July, 1844. On the first fire of the soldiers, no ball entered his heart. He looked up, but with no spirit of revenge, no aspect of defiance,—only sat upon his countenance the desire to pass at once into the region where no death is.

"Pity me," said he, "and fire here,"—putting his hand upon his heart. Two balls then entered his body, and Placido fell.

As Wordsworth said of Toussaint, so may it be said of Placido,—

> "Thou hast left behind thee
> Powers that will work for thee; air, earth, and skies.
> There's not a breathing of the common wind
> That will forget thee; thou hast great allies,
> Thy friends are exultations, agonies,

And love, and man's unconquerable mind."

The charge against Placido was, that he was at the head of a conspiracy to overthrow slavery in his native island. Blessings on thee, Placido! Nor didst thou fail of thy mission. Did the martyrs, stake-bound, fail of theirs? As the Lord liveth, Cuba shall yet be free.

That Placido was at the head of this conspiracy there is not a doubt; but what his plans in detail were, I know not; the means of acquiring them are not within my reach. Nevertheless, from the treatment throughout of the Cuban authorities towards Placido, we may safely conclude that Placido's plan in detail evinced no lack of ability to originate and execute, nor of that sagacity which should mark a revolutionary leader. Placido hated slavery with a hatred intensified by the remembrance of wrongs which a loving and loved mother had borne. The iron, too, had entered into his own soul; and he had been a daily witness of scenes such as torment itself could scarcely equal, nor the pit itself outdo. Call you this extravagance? You will not,—should you but study a single chapter in the history of Cuban slavery.

Do you honor Kossuth?—then forget not him who is worthy to stand side by side with Hungary's illustrious son.

What may be the destiny of Cuba in the future near at hand, I will not venture to predict. What may be her *ultimate* destiny is written in the fact that,—"God hath no attribute which, in a contest between the oppressed and the oppressor, can take sides with the latter."

This sketch, though hastily written, and meagre in detail as it must necessarily be, will show, at least, by the quotations of poetry introduced, that God hath not given to one race alone, all intellectual and moral greatness.

Prof. William G. Allen

END OF VOL. I.

Lector House believes that a society develops through a two-fold approach of continuous learning and adaptation, which is derived from the study of classic literary works spread across the historic timeline of literature records. Therefore, we aim at reviving, repairing and redeveloping all those inaccessible or damaged but historically as well as culturally important literature across subjects so that the future generations may have an opportunity to study and learn from past works to embark upon a journey of creating a better future.

This book is a result of an effort made by Lector House towards making a contribution to the preservation and repair of original ancient works which might hold historical significance to the approach of continuous learning across subjects.

HAPPY READING & LEARNING!

LECTOR HOUSE LLP
E-MAIL: lectorpublishing@gmail.com

Lightning Source UK Ltd.
Milton Keynes UK
UKHW010647090820
367908UK00002B/406